Transforming Teaching With Generative AI

A Comprehensive Guide for Educators

Nick Gaspar

Foreword by Tazin Daniels

Teachers College Press
Teachers College, Columbia University

Published by Teachers College Press,® 1234 Amsterdam Avenue, New York, NY 10027

Library of Congress Cataloging-in-Publication Data is available at loc.gov

ISBN 978-0-8077-8740-3 (paper)
ISBN 978-0-8077-8741-0 (hardcover)
ISBN 978-0-8077-8325-2 (ebook)

Printed on acid-free paper
Manufactured in the United States of America

For everyone who trusted my instincts when
a strange-sounding new tool first appeared.
Your encouragement made all the difference.

Contents

Foreword

I met Nick Gaspar when we were both recruited to serve on the University of Michigan's Generative AI Advisory Committee. From the moment we sat in that meeting together, it was clear that Nick was already thinking 10 steps ahead, offering a vision that challenged us all to think more expansively about the future of AI in higher education. His deep knowledge of educational technology, his collaborative spirit, and his commitment to making generative AI accessible for all educators stood out immediately. He wasn't there to gatekeep knowledge; he openly shared resources, presentations, tools, and strategies with everyone around him, making sure no one felt left behind in this rapidly changing landscape.

For educators today, the emergence of generative AI is as daunting as it is thrilling. They feel caught between curiosity and panic, eager to explore what these tools can do but unsure where to begin or how to engage in ways that align with their personal values. In many places, faculty have limited access to institutional support, and most workshops and webinars fall short in terms of time for exploration and disciplinary nuance. What they truly need is a coach, someone who understands both AI and the challenges of teaching, can meet them where they are, and guide them step-by-step. That is exactly what this book offers: a thoughtful, practical, and values-driven resource that empowers educators to engage with AI critically, ethically, and creatively, no matter their discipline, institution, or starting point.

I've had the privilege of working with Nick on several projects, including coleading the Teaching with GenAI Learning Community that supported 60 University of Michigan faculty across disciplines in advancing their AI skills and copresenting at the 2024 Michigan GET-IT Summit for high school girls exploring the future of AI. Nick's excitement for AI in education is contagious. I've seen firsthand how his practical advice, clear guidance, and encouragement empowered faculty to make meaningful progress on projects that are both feasible and valuable. He leads by example, never shying away from challenges, whether it's answering the toughest questions in a room full of skeptics or sharing a personal story—like how he first used AI to find a panini recipe—to make a complex topic more approachable. I always look forward to hearing about the latest project Nick is working on or the new tool he's exploring. He's as humble as he is knowledgeable, always exchanging ideas with others, which is probably why he knows so much about this field.

In this book, Nick combines a strategic mindset with a sharp understanding of the human side of teaching and learning. He sees the big picture, the systemic shifts AI is catalyzing in higher education, and yet he never loses sight of the classroom, the learner, and the relationships that make education meaningful. He understands that the most urgent questions about AI are not just technical; they are ethical, pedagogical, and profoundly human. That's why this book does not just teach you *how* to use GenAI tools. It invites you to ask *why*, and it equips you with the frameworks, case studies, and reflection prompts to do so.

What makes this book so special is its blend of practicality and perspective. It is structured in bite-sized chapters that encourage reflection, experimentation, and small steps forward, perfect for educators who feel too overwhelmed to know where to start. Nick's voice is like a trusted colleague sitting beside you, gently guiding you through each activity, sharing scripts for conversations with students, and offering just enough technical knowledge to help you have a smart, informed conversation about AI without feeling buried in jargon.

You will find practical examples from across disciplines; nuanced discussions of bias, equity, and accessibility; and clear strategies for maintaining academic integrity in a world where the five-paragraph essay may no longer suffice. Nick helps you think critically about how to leverage GenAI to increase creativity, free up time for deeper engagement with students, and personalize learning, while avoiding the common traps of overreliance, inequity, and bias.

Whether you are a complete beginner or a seasoned AI experimenter, you will come away from this book with concrete strategies, a deeper understanding of the issues at stake, and, perhaps most importantly, the confidence to take your next step. In the end, this is more than a book about technology; it is an invitation to reimagine what education can be in an AI-infused world.

I am honored to introduce *Transforming Teaching with Generative AI* to you. I hope it sparks your curiosity, supports your practice, and helps you feel less alone in navigating these uncharted waters. But don't just read this book. Experiment, reflect, and return to it as a trusted companion. With Nick as your guide, you are in good hands.

—Dr. Tazin Daniels
Associate Director, Center for Research on Learning and Teaching, University of Michigan
May 2025

Acknowledgments

Writing this book has been a journey shaped by countless conversations, collaborations, and a good deal of patience from those around me. I want to begin with my family. To my wife, Meghann, thank you for your love and unwavering support through the long hours, the weekends and vacations with my laptop open, and the evenings when my mind was still half in a chapter. To my father, Edward; my brothers, Brian and Timothy; and my grandmother, Barbara: your encouragement and belief in me over the years have been a constant source of strength. And to all the members of my extended family who have supported me along the way, I am grateful for your love and support.

I am indebted to my colleagues in Online and Digital Education at the University of Michigan–Flint. Carson Waites, Brandon Blinkenberg, and Jeff Drake, along with the entire ODE team, shaped my experience in ways that deeply informed this book. The projects we undertook, the challenges we worked through, and the experiments we ran together all sharpened my understanding of how generative AI could impact teaching and learning.

I'm also grateful to all academic leadership at UM-Flint, especially deans Donna Fry, Cynthia McCurren, Yener Kandogan, and Christopher Pearson and their executive committees. Your forward-thinking and proactive approach inspired me and drove the development of many resources that helped position UM-Flint as a leader in this space. It was your recognition of the importance this technology would have in higher education, and the autonomy you gave us to pursue the best ways to support our campus, that made this work possible.

Ravi Pendse and Robert Jones deserve special thanks for their leadership and vision in integrating GenAI tools across the entirety of U-M, and for including me on the Generative AI Advisory Committee. I am also grateful to my colleagues who served alongside me as part of GAIA. This was one of the most valuable and transformative experiences of my career. I'd also like to thank everyone in ITS Teaching and Learning and at the Center for Research on Learning and Teaching at U-M. Those of you I've had the chance to work with have provided a wonderful partnership that resulted in innovative resources and programs that have helped drive our institution forward in integrating AI in teaching and learning.

I'd also like to extend gratitude to the many faculty and students whose curiosity, resilience, and engagement shaped so many of the examples included here.

Their willingness to experiment, ask tough questions, and embrace change gave life to the ideas explored throughout these chapters.

Special thanks to Punya Mishra and Mathew Koehler, whose development of the TPACK framework continues to influence how I think about technology and teaching. I also want to acknowledge the wider community of scholars and practitioners, people like Ethan Mollick, Bryan Alexander, and researchers at my very own University of Michigan and Stanford's Institute for Human-Centered AI.

Thanks to everyone I've worked with at Teachers College Press. Particularly Emily Spangler, Alyssa Jordan, Sudeshna Dasgupta, Nancy Power, John Bylander, and anyone else who helped shepherd this book from idea to print. From my discovery to the careful attention of a team that came together to help a first-time author, I could not have done this without your guidance. Thank you as well for your patience with my endless questions throughout the process.

Finally, my friend and colleague Tazin Daniels. From our first connection on the GAIA committee to leading teaching circles with more faculty than we ever imagined, your companionship has been a true gift. Thank you for listening to my ideas, for sharing your own, and for accepting my invitation to contribute to this work. I will always carry the lessons and inspiration from working alongside you.

Introduction

Standing at the Precipice of Change

As you begin to read this book, let's reflect on our position within the larger timeline that represents humanity and our relationship to technology. We truly are members of the lucky few.

Think about this: For nearly a million years after discovering fire, our ancestors used it simply for warmth and protection. Then one mind discovered that placing food in the flames made it tastier and easier to digest—a culinary revolution that transformed human nutrition and development. Hundreds of thousands more years would pass before someone realized that throwing certain shiny rocks into that same fire could produce metals for tools far more precise than stone implements. This insight changed everything about how humans could shape their world.

Fast-forward through thousands of years that brought agriculture, writing, mathematics, and the printing press, each a revolution. Then someone observed that boiling water produces steam with enough force to do work or spin a turbine. Welcome to the Industrial Revolution, where the pace of change began to accelerate dramatically.

And then we were off to the races.

These technological revolutions, developed across human history, initially occurred across vast time spans that slowly shortened with each breakthrough. Most humans who ever lived experienced perhaps one such revolution in their lifetime, if they were lucky. Yet those of us living today are witnessing advancements at an almost unimaginable pace.

You might reflect on the progression from vacuum tubes to transistors, the miniaturization of technology through integrated circuits leading to personal computers. Then came the internet, creating a global communication network, followed by the mobile revolution that put those computers in our pockets. Each of these technologies had to converge to make further advancements possible. Before we could develop artificial intelligence, we needed processing power, storage capacity, and methods to transmit vast amounts of information quickly.

But it's the mobile revolution that truly sets this current transformation apart. One of the primary reasons tools like ChatGPT, Claude, Gemini, DeepSeek, and Perplexity have gained such widespread popularity is their accessibility and ease of use—all made possible by smartphones. The mobile revolution made AI scalable at a global level, placing the power of artificial intelligence literally in the palm of our hands.

If we can come together as educators to navigate this transformation thoughtfully, we will have an unprecedented opportunity to make teaching more efficient and accelerate learning for the betterment of both society and our local communities. More people will have access to education than at any other time in human history, helping us address persistent challenges like poverty, illiteracy, and economic instability.

The chapters that follow will equip you to integrate AI into your teaching practice effectively. To help guide that integration, this book leans on two frameworks that many educators already know and trust: Technological Pedagogical and Content Knowledge (TPACK) and Transparency in Learning and Teaching (TILT). TPACK is a model for thinking about how teaching content, pedagogy, and technology intersect. It helps us make decisions about where AI tools fit meaningfully within what we're already doing in the classroom. TILT, on the other hand, encourages clarity around assignment goals, tasks, and success criteria—an essential consideration when AI enters the mix.

The ideas in this book also build on a growing body of research and reflection happening across the field. Scholars like Ethan Mollick, Bryan Alexander, and researchers at institutions such as Stanford's Institute for Human-Centered Artificial Intelligence and the University of Toronto's Schwartz Reisman Institute are asking big questions about AI's role in education, access, and ethics (Alexander, 2023).

Bryan Alexander, a futurist and researcher, explores the future of higher education and the impact of AI in his book *Academia Next: The Futures of Higher Education* (Alexander, 2020). He has been tracking AI and education since the 1990s, examining its potential impacts on academia (Alexander, 2023).

Those who embrace and master these tools now will find themselves in a far better position in two to three years than those who shun or ignore them. We stand at a pivotal moment in education, one where the decisions we make today will shape learning experiences for generations to come.

Welcome to the AI revolution. Let's begin.

CHAPTER 1

Foundations of Generative AI

Introduction to AI and Its Evolution in Education

INTRODUCTION AND KEY CONCEPTS

Introduction

The first time I ever used generative AI, I instantly knew the focus of the department I lead was going to shift forever. In November 2022, one of my staff members, an instructional designer named Carson, dropped into Slack a note about this new tool he'd been experimenting with called ChatGPT. "Hmm, weird name," I thought. I didn't quite understand it at first, but I asked Carson to keep an eye on it in case this was going to turn into something bigger. If only I knew what was in store for my department, and higher education as a whole, when I tapped the Send button in Slack, our team's messaging platform.

Fast-forward to today, when AI is already reshaping the landscape of higher education in ways both subtle and transformative. It automates routine tasks, freeing up educators to focus on the human aspects of teaching. Tasks like mentoring, problem solving, and guiding a student's growth are now more accessible. These are the tasks that require higher-level thinking and passion to help students succeed in their academic journey. If you've ever wished that you could employ real-world personalized learning strategies in your classroom but never had the time or energy to do so for the 30, 60, or 90 students you're educating in a semester, that wish could now be a reality. By understanding and leveraging this technology effectively, you'll have the opportunity to help students who might otherwise feel lost in a crowded lecture hall.

The use of AI in education has been evolving quickly, and we are now at a critical moment. AI's role in supporting learning started with early attempts at computer-assisted instruction, but recent breakthroughs in deep learning and access to vast datasets have brought generative AI to the forefront. Tools like ChatGPT and Claude are reshaping how we approach education. They are pushing us to rethink the educator's role in modern education.

In this chapter, we will explore the key technologies behind generative AI, starting with the basics of machine learning and the complexities of natural language processing. My goal is to help you understand what generative AI is, how it works, and where it's currently making an impact in education.

As we investigate these concepts, I hope you'll begin to see the potential, not just as a technological evolution but to reclaim some of what you have lost in recent history: time, engagement, and the space for creativity. Generative AI offers us a chance to rethink our approach, to help educators and students alike, in a way that's practical and, most importantly, human centered.

Understanding Generative AI

Before we get into the details, I'd like to make sure there is an understanding of the key concepts and terms that will be used throughout the book. Generative AI draws on many technologies, theories, and frameworks that may not be immediately familiar to everyone. By defining these foundational terms now, we can establish a common language that will make the rest of our discussion more impactful.

Understanding concepts like machine learning, natural language processing, and transformers provides the foundation we need to fully engage with this content. This chapter will break down these key definitions in a straightforward way so that you're prepared with this knowledge before we move into more complex topics. With this background, you'll be in a better position to see how generative AI can effectively reshape educational practices. Table 1.1 outlines these key concepts.

Table 1.1. Key Concepts

Term	Definition
Artificial Intelligence (AI)	AI refers to the ability of digital systems, such as computers or robots, to perform tasks typically associated with intelligent beings. These tasks encompass a wide range of capabilities, from learning and reasoning to understanding language and problem solving. AI systems can adapt to new situations, recognize complex patterns, and make decisions based on vast amounts of data.
Example: Imagine a smart home system that learns your daily routines. It adjusts the temperature, turns lights on and off, and even suggests grocery lists based on your habits, all without explicit programming for each task.	
Machine Learning (ML)	ML is a core component of AI that focuses on developing algorithms capable of learning from data. Instead of following explicit programming instructions, ML models improve their performance over time by identifying patterns and gaining insights from the information they process.
Example: Think of an ML model as a novice chess player who improves by analyzing thousands of chess games. With each game it studies, it learns new strategies and becomes better at predicting effective moves, eventually developing its own playing style.	

(*continued*)

Table 1.1. *(continued)*

Datasets	Datasets are the lifeblood of AI systems, providing the raw information from which these systems learn. They can be structured (organized in predefined formats like databases) or unstructured (like collections of text or images without a specific organization). The quality and diversity of datasets significantly influence an AI's performance and capabilities.
Example: Think about the training a sommelier would have to go through. A structured dataset would be like a detailed wine catalog with specific attributes for each wine. An unstructured dataset, on the other hand, would be akin to a collection of wine reviews, tasting notes, and vineyard descriptions from various sources.	
Natural Language Processing (NLP)	NLP is the field of AI dedicated to enabling computers to understand, interpret, and generate human language. It bridges the gap between machine language and human communication, making it possible for AI systems to engage in tasks ranging from translation to sentiment analysis.
Example: NLP is like a translator who listens to someone speaking in a different language and then responds in your language, allowing you to have a conversation even if you don't speak the same language. In our real-world case, NLP is translating between machine language and your human language.	
Token	A token is the smallest unit of meaning that an AI model processes. Tokens can be words, parts of words, or even individual characters, depending on the model's design. The process of breaking text into these units is called *tokenization*, a crucial step in enabling AI to analyze and generate language.
Example: Consider how you might explain the meaning of a sentence to a child learning to read. You'd break it down into words, and sometimes parts of words, to help them understand. Tokenization works similarly, breaking text into manageable pieces that the AI can process and understand.	
Transformer	Transformers are a revolutionary architecture in machine learning, particularly adept at processing sequential data like language. Unlike earlier models that analyzed text linearly, transformers can consider the entire context simultaneously, allowing for more nuanced understanding and generation of language.
Example: Imagine a master detective who can instantly connect clues from different parts of a case to solve complex mysteries. Similarly, a transformer model can link words and phrases from various parts of a text to derive deeper meanings and generate more contextually relevant responses.	
Large Language Model (LLM)	LLMs are AI systems designed to understand and generate humanlike text. Trained on diverse sources such as books, articles, and websites, these models can predict word sequences, answer questions, assist with writing tasks, and engage in conversations. Their vast knowledge base allows them to tackle a wide range of language-related tasks with impressive accuracy.

(continued)

Table 1.1. (*continued*)

Example: Picture a hyperintelligent digital librarian with instant access to millions of books and articles. When you ask this librarian a question, it doesn't just recite facts; it synthesizes information from countless sources to provide a comprehensive, well-reasoned answer.	
Generative Pre-Trained Transformer (GPT)	GPTs are sophisticated language models trained on enormous datasets to grasp the intricacies of human communication. By analyzing vast amounts of text, these models can generate coherent, contextually relevant responses to a wide array of prompts. GPTs power many modern AI applications, from chatbots to content creation tools.
Example: Imagine having a conversation with a multilingual poet who has read every book ever written. A GPT model can similarly engage in discussions on countless topics, craft poems in various styles, or even help with translation, all by drawing on its extensive "reading" of human-generated text.	
Generative Models (GenAI)	Generative models are a subset of machine learning algorithms. They learn patterns and structures from training data to create new, original content that mimics the characteristics of that data. These models can produce a wide variety of outputs, from images and text to computer code and even music.
Example: Think of a generative model as a digital artist who has studied thousands of Van Gogh paintings. After learning the artist's unique style, brushstrokes, and color palette, it can create new paintings that capture the essence of Van Gogh's work—without directly copying any existing piece.	
Prompt	A prompt is the initial input given to an AI model to guide its output. It can be a question, a statement, or any text that provides context for the AI to generate a relevant response. The art of crafting effective prompts, known as "prompt engineering," is crucial for obtaining desired results from AI models.
Example: Prompts are like the opening line of an improv scene. Just as that line sets the stage for the actors, guiding the direction of their performance, a well-crafted prompt steers an AI's response, helping it generate more relevant and focused output.	
Transfer Learning	This technique allows AI models to apply knowledge gained from one task to a different but related task. This approach significantly reduces the amount of data and computational power needed to train models for new applications, making AI development more efficient and accessible.
Example: A chef has worked to master French cuisine. When learning to cook Italian food, that chef doesn't start from scratch, but rather applies their knowledge of ingredients, cooking techniques, and flavor combinations to quickly adapt to the new cuisine.	

(*continued*)

Table 1.1. (*continued*)

Multimodal AI	This is an AI that can understand and work with different types of information, such as text, images, audio, or video, all at the same time. This versatility allows it to interpret complex scenarios more holistically, mirroring the way humans integrate multiple senses to understand their environment.
Example: Consider an AI assistant helping a chef in the kitchen. It can read recipe instructions, recognize ingredients from images, understand verbal commands, and even analyze cooking videos, all at once. It could then provide comprehensive guidance throughout the cooking process.	
Hallucination	AI hallucination occurs when a model generates information that is not grounded in its training data or the given input. This can result in plausible-sounding but factually incorrect or nonsensical outputs. Hallucinations are a significant challenge in AI development, particularly for applications requiring high accuracy.
Example: Imagine asking a highly knowledgeable friend about a topic they've never studied. They might confidently provide an answer that sounds reasonable but is entirely made up. AI hallucinations work similarly; the model generates a response that fits the pattern of what it thinks is expected, even if the information is incorrect.	
AI-Assisted Learning	AI-Assisted Learning leverages artificial intelligence to enhance educational experiences. These systems can provide personalized feedback, adapt content to individual learning styles, and offer tailored practice exercises. By analyzing a student's performance and learning patterns, AI can create a more efficient, engaging, and effective learning environment.
Example: Picture a virtual tutor that explains concepts and adapts its style based on your responses. If you struggle with visual explanations, it might switch to auditory examples. If you excel in one area, it can then introduce more challenging material. This personalized approach is what AI-assisted learning aims to achieve on a large scale.	

COMMON AI AND EDUCATION TECHNOLOGY TOOLS

To help you get a sense of the AI tools referenced throughout this book, Table 1.2 offers a snapshot of some of the most common ones, with brief descriptions and a few key features to help you decide if they might fit your needs.

Mechanisms Behind Generative AI

As we get started, let's gain an understanding of the mechanisms that drive generative AI. Specifically, we'll look at how machine learning and natural language processing influence how GenAI functions. Let's break down these components to give you a clearer picture of how they work together in driving this technology.

Table 1.2. Common Generative AI Tools and Their Notable Features

Tool	Description	Notable Features
ChatGPT (OpenAI)	Versatile conversational model used for writing, brainstorming, tutoring, and more	• Strong dialogue abilities • Custom GPTs for tailored use • Widely integrated
Claude (Anthropic)	Conversational AI that emphasizes safe, steerable output	• Handles long documents well • Clear, structured replies • Focus on reliability
DeepSeek	Open-source LLM with a focus on education and programming support	• Free to use • Code-aware responses • Growing support in academic settings
Gemini (Google)	Multimodal AI that handles text, images, and code	• Strong research capabilities • Tied to Google ecosystem • Visual input support
LLaMA (Meta)	Open-source LLM with solid performance and low implementation cost	• Free and modifiable • Strong language reasoning • Ideal for experimentation
Perplexity	Research-focused assistant that cites sources and offers summaries	• Source attribution • Live web access • Fast information lookup
Deep Research (OpenAI)	AI-powered research assistant designed to synthesize academic sources and answer complex questions	• Cites sources directly • Great for academic deep dives • Ideal for exploring nuanced topics
DreamBox Learning	Adaptive learning platform focused on K–8 math	• Real-time student adaptation • Visual learning tools • Standards-aligned
Google Translate	Language translation tool useful for multilingual classrooms	• Real-time translation • Wide language support • Free and easy to use
Gradescope	Grading platform that uses AI to assist with rubric-based assessments	• Auto-grading for quizzes • Group similar answers • Annotated feedback
Grammarly	Writing assistant for grammar, clarity, and tone	• Real-time editing • Tone suggestions

(continued)

Table 1.2. (*continued*)

Tool	Description	Notable Features
Khanmigo (Khan Academy)	AI assistant embedded in Khan Academy for tutoring and feedback	• Practice problem generator • Personalized student help
Quizlet	Study tool that generates flash cards and quizzes from text	• Auto-generates content • Supports spaced repetition • Mobile-friendly
Turnitin	Academic integrity platform for plagiarism detection	• AI writing detection • Integration with learning management systems (LMSs) • Detailed originality reports
Whisper (OpenAI)	Speech-to-text model that transcribes spoken audio	• Transcription • Multilingual support • Useful for accessibility

Machine Learning

Machine learning is a way for computers to learn from examples instead of following fixed rules. For instance, by looking at thousands of emails labeled "spam" or "not spam," a computer can start to recognize patterns and make its own decisions about new messages. This kind of training, called supervised learning, helps form the foundation for how AI understands and organizes information.

When it comes to generative AI, other learning methods are often more important. Unsupervised and self-supervised learning let AI explore patterns in huge amounts of data without needing clear labels. This makes them great for creative tasks, like writing or summarizing, where the structure matters more than any specific right answer.

Most generative AI tools use a technique called *deep learning*. These systems rely on layered networks (called *neural networks*) that loosely mimic how the human brain processes information. They break down complex inputs, like sentences, into smaller parts, find patterns, and gradually piece together a response that makes sense. It's this process that allows ChatGPT to generate paragraphs, respond to questions, and summarize articles.

The Role of Natural Language Processing

Natural language processing, or NLP, is what allows computers to understand and respond to human language. If you've ever typed a question into a chatbot or asked a virtual assistant to set a timer, you've used NLP in action.

Think of it like this: NLP is how we teach computers to listen and talk like us. The goal isn't just recognizing words but making sense of them in context. Early attempts at this relied on long lists of grammar rules, like handing a computer a textbook and hoping it could carry on a conversation. But language is messy, full of exceptions and nuance, and those rule-based systems didn't get us very far.

Today's NLP systems use machine learning instead. By analyzing massive amounts of text, computers learn the patterns of human language—how words relate to one another, how tone changes meaning, and how context shapes interpretation. That shift, from memorizing rules to learning from experience, is what makes modern NLP so powerful. NLP techniques help AI pick up not just the grammar and structure of your words but also the meaning behind them. That's why ChatGPT, Siri, and Alexa can now produce responses that sound natural, stay on topic, and even catch a hint of sarcasm when needed.

Why This Is Important

Natural language processing serves as a communication bridge between computers and humans. Comprehending NLP helps us understand how this bridge is constructed and maintained. Without it, our attempts to interact with AI would resemble a conversation where neither party understands the other's language. By understanding how this works, developers can create AI systems that offer more natural, engaging, and helpful interactions with users. This could be an AI tutor capable of understanding a student's questions and providing clear explanations, or a human resource application that allows you to simulate tough conversations.

As we train AI to comprehend and produce human language, we need to make sure it uses language responsibly and ethically. This involves avoiding biases, respecting privacy, and making sure the AI communicates positively and doesn't disseminate misinformation. In addition to this, NLP can make technology more accessible to people who might otherwise have difficulties using it. For example, voice-activated assistants can help those with physical disabilities, while translation services break down language barriers. NLP allows us to enhance and expand these types of services, making technology more inclusive for everyone.

Generative AI in Action

Generative AI models, like OpenAI's GPT series, combine machine learning with NLP in a powerful way. These models are typically trained on vast amounts of text, from books and websites to other written forms, to capture the statistical relationships between words, phrases, and even broader topics. After training, the model can generate new content by predicting one word after another based on the context it has learned.

A model like OpenAI's GPT-4o creates text by predicting one word at a time based on patterns it has learned during training. It uses advanced mathematics and neural networks to produce text that's coherent, contextually appropriate, and stylistically aligned with your input. While it doesn't truly "understand" what it's writing, its ability to mimic humanlike responses is the result of processing an extraordinary amount of language data and leveraging powerful computational tools like transformers and attention mechanisms. We'll learn more about those pieces in the next chapter.

A key part of GPT-4o's text generation is probabilities. When predicting the next word, the model doesn't just pick one option outright, it calculates probabilities for all possible next words and chooses the most likely one. After the initial training, GPT-4o undergoes a process called *fine tuning* where it's refined using specific datasets or guided feedback. This feedback often requires human reviewers to provide examples of what good answers look like, so the model learns how to prioritize clarity and relevance of its output. This feedback also helps it to adjust when the responses it gives are inaccurate or unhelpful.

Here's a simple example of how ChatGPT can answer questions. The scenario involves a student asking it questions about a topic, say, photosynthesis, and ChatGPT responding as if it's a knowledgeable tutor.

User Prompt: Can you explain the basic process of photosynthesis?
ChatGPT: Sure! Photosynthesis is the process by which green plants, algae, and some bacteria convert light energy from the sun into chemical energy stored in glucose. The process primarily occurs in the chloroplasts of plant cells, which contain a pigment called chlorophyll.

In simple terms:

- Plants take in carbon dioxide (CO_2) from the air and water (H_2O) from the soil.
- Using sunlight as energy, they transform these into glucose ($C_6H_{12}O_6$) and oxygen (O_2).
- The overall equation is $6CO_2 + 6H_2O$ + light energy $\rightarrow$ $C_6H_{12}O_6 + 6O_26CO_2 + 6H_2O$ + light energy $\rightarrow C_6H_{12}O_6 + 6O_26CO_2 + 6H_2O$ + light energy $\rightarrow C_6\,H_{12}\,O_6 + 6O_2$.

This is how plants produce food for themselves and release oxygen into the atmosphere, which is essential for life on Earth.

When ChatGPT generated the response represented above, it starts by interpreting your prompt: "Can you explain the basic process of photosynthesis?" It identified that the request was for a clear and basic explanation, not overly technical but still accurate. The system then searched its trained knowledge base, which contains immense amounts of text data on scientific concepts like photosynthesis. It retrieved the most relevant information and ranked the details by importance, prioritizing foundational ideas about how plants convert light energy into glucose and oxygen.

Next, ChatGPT began structuring the response. Internally, it applies natural language processing techniques to break the information into manageable segments and maintain a logical, smooth flow. It used clear phrasing to describe the steps of photosynthesis, emphasizing actions like "plants take in carbon dioxide" and "they transform these into glucose." Additionally, it decided to include the chemical equation as supplemental detail, demonstrating an understanding that some users might value a more technical layer of explanation based on how that information is represented in its training data.

Throughout the process, ChatGPT relied on fine-tuned models to adapt its tone, language, and structure for clarity and engagement. It chose simple words to make the explanation accessible to a wide audience. At the same time, it aimed to highlight the relevance of photosynthesis by linking it to oxygen production and life on Earth. This balance between accuracy and user-friendly delivery is a core part of how ChatGPT operates when responding to questions.

APPLICATIONS IN EDUCATIONAL SETTINGS

The current applications in educational settings are as diverse as they are transformative, touching everything from personalized learning experiences to content creation and curation. These applications of AI in education align with key principles of the Technological Pedagogical and Content Knowledge (TPACK) framework, which we'll explore in detail in Chapter 3. TPACK provides a valuable lens for understanding how technology like AI works together with teaching strategies and subject expertise. When you are evaluating AI tools for your classroom, considering how they complement your pedagogical approach and content goals helps create more effective learning experiences.

In this section, we'll introduce these topics, offering a glimpse into how AI is reshaping classrooms and addressing both its benefits and challenges. Each of these areas will be explored in greater depth in the chapters ahead, but for now, let's examine the foundation of these innovations and their impact on modern education.

Automated Grading and Feedback

One of the most practical applications of AI in education is automated grading and feedback. These systems leverage AI to streamline the assessment process, offering instant evaluations of student work. From analyzing essays for grammar and structure to flagging plagiarism and grading quizzes, these tools are transforming how we manage the often time-consuming task of evaluation. By providing consistent and actionable feedback, these systems empower students to improve their work while freeing up teachers to focus on more personalized and impactful aspects of instruction.

Tools like Turnitin, Grammarly, and Gradescope have become essential in classrooms, offering educators a way to evaluate student work more efficiently. These systems can grade multiple-choice quizzes instantly, flag plagiarism in essays, and provide real-time feedback on grammar, style, and even the structure of written assignments.

Gradescope uses machine learning to assess handwritten and typed assignments. It can identify patterns in student answers, making grading faster and more consistent. Grammarly, widely used by students and educators alike, offers detailed feedback on tone, word choice, and clarity, giving students the opportunity to revise their work before submission. These tools go beyond simple corrections and act as a supplemental guide to improve writing skills.

Moreover, AI can analyze patterns across an entire class to identify trends, meaning that if you find students are struggling with a particular question or concept, you can more readily adjust your instruction.

Despite these benefits, automated grading tools are not without their challenges. AI systems lack the understanding of a human grader, the full context of the course material, and can struggle to evaluate creativity, critical thinking, or the meaning behind a student's work. Consider:

- An essay with flawless grammar but weak arguments might receive higher marks than one with stronger ideas but minor errors.
- AI systems can misinterpret cultural references or unique writing styles, leading to inappropriate feedback.

Should AI Assign Grades?

I can't stress enough that while AI is a helpful tool for providing feedback, it shouldn't be the sole determinant of grades. Assigning grades requires a holistic evaluation that considers creativity, effort, and context, qualities that AI cannot fully understand. Instead, AI should act as a support system for you, reducing your workload and offering initial insights that can be reviewed and refined by a human grader.

Imagine you're teaching an introductory writing course, and your 120 students have just submitted their first major essay. You're faced with a mountain of grading that looms over you, threatening to swallow up your evenings and weekends. In a moment of practicality, you decide to use ChatGPT to speed things along. A tool like ChatGPT can easily assess the essays, flag grammatical issues, evaluate structure, and even give a preliminary score based on a rubric you upload. Sounds like the perfect solution to lighten the load, right? Let's take a closer look at what this really means.

For this scenario, consider three students: Sarah, John, and Alex.

Sarah's essay is technically flawless. It checks every box on your rubric with clear structure, proper grammar, and a well-defined thesis statement. The ChatGPT assigns Sarah a high score, and from a purely rubric-based standpoint, it seems well deserved. But as you read it, you can't help but feel something is missing. The essay, though technically competent, is uninspired. It plays it safe and lacks any real depth or originality. Sarah has followed all the rules but hasn't taken any risks or injected her own voice.

Let's turn to John's writing. John's essay is less polished; there are a few grammatical errors, and some of the arguments are a bit scattered. But John took a creative leap, exploring an unusual interpretation of the prompt that makes you stop and think. The AI, however, doesn't recognize the value of John's creativity. It strictly looks at the rubric, structure, grammar, adherence to the prompt, and deducts points for the imperfections. John ends up with a mediocre score, even though the essay shows engagement and originality that could be worth rewarding.

Take Alex's case. Her essay is messy. The grammar is inconsistent, and the structure is somewhat disorganized. But you can feel the passion behind it. Alex is wrestling with the material in a personal way, making connections that are raw but meaningful. The AI, however, doesn't see effort or intention; it sees errors and a lack of clarity. Alex's score is low, because the AI simply can't appreciate someone pushing themselves to express a difficult idea or the journey they've taken to get this far.

And that's really the problem. When AI grades these essays, it's looking strictly through the lens of your rubric metrics: structure, grammar, adherence to the writing prompt. Sarah's essay, with its technical precision, comes out on top because it ticks all the boxes, after all. But John, who tried to make a creative leap, and Alex, who poured real heart into the paper, got average or even poor scores. The AI isn't wrong according to the rubric, but it's incomplete in its judgment. The grades end up looking fair on the surface, technically correct, but they completely miss the underlying value of those student efforts.

Grading is about more than just technical accuracy; it's about recognizing creativity, effort, and the individual journey of each student. AI can help streamline parts of the grading process, but it lacks the human ability to see beyond the surface, to understand the risks a student took, the progress they've made, and the personal stakes they have in their work. Without that, the grades become mere numbers devoid of the story behind them, and we risk losing the very essence of what makes teaching and learning meaningful.

Another important issue is the inconsistency in how AI tools generate numerical scores. Tools like ChatGPT are designed to provide probabilistic outputs, meaning they often "guess" numerical values when it comes to grading. Feed the same essay into the system twice, and you'll end up with two different scores. This inconsistency is a serious flaw when it comes to academic evaluation. Grades aren't meant to be arbitrary numbers; they're intended to be a representation of a student's understanding, effort, and growth. If an AI can't reliably assign the same grade to the same work every time, it undermines the very purpose of grading.

Students deserve fair and consistent evaluation of their efforts, and when an AI tool arbitrarily changes its assessment, it risks eroding trust, not just in the grading process but in the educational system as a whole.

Personalized Learning Strategies

One of the most promising ways AI is transforming education is through personalized learning experiences. Generative AI and machine learning technologies create individualized learning paths that adapt to each student's needs, offering a level of personalization that was once impossible in traditional classrooms. With AI, every student can have a digital learning companion that continuously adapts based on their strengths, struggles, and learning preferences, effectively tailoring their educational journey.

Creating Individual Learning Paths

Models such as those found in products like DreamBox Learning or Khan Academy have the ability to analyze a student's interactions, such as the questions they ask, their engagement levels, and even their response times. With these data points, AI can develop a unique learning plan that targets specific areas for improvement while reinforcing strengths. For instance, if a student is struggling with fraction division, DreamBox might provide additional step-by-step exercises focusing specifically on dividing fractions. If the student still finds it challenging, the AI could switch to a visual method, using interactive fraction bars to show how division works visually. Alternatively, it could suggest real-world applications, like using recipes to illustrate how dividing fractions is used in cooking.

The content generated by these tools is highly adaptable. If a student excels in a topic, the system can accelerate their learning, introduce more challenging material, or shift the focus to a new skill. This dynamic way of learning is especially effective for diverse classrooms, including those that might consist of nontraditional students, such as adult learners with different backgrounds and experiences. These enhanced learning paths empower students to learn at their own pace so they neither feel left behind nor held back regardless of their prior knowledge or unique circumstances.

Identifying Strengths and Areas for Improvement

AI revolutionizes educational assessment by providing continuous, formative evaluation rather than limited snapshots of student knowledge. These systems:

- Track student interactions in real time, precisely identifying strengths and weaknesses.
- Automatically adapt learning pathways based on performance patterns.

- Provide customized support, for example, extra practice with hints for struggling areas.

For educators, AI tools deliver:

- Comprehensive classroom visibility.
- User-friendly data analysis.
- The ability to automate administrative tasks that free up time for meaningful student engagement.

The Impact on Engagement and Learning Outcomes

It's possible that personalized AI-driven learning paths can significantly boost student engagement and achievement by:

- Matching content to individual learning pace, preferences, and personality.
- Delivering educational materials tailored to student interests.
- Confirming concept mastery before moving on to more challenging material.

As we progress through this book, we'll examine specific applications of AI in creating these personalized learning environments. The potential extends beyond improved scores or teaching efficiency. AI is redefining education itself, making learning more responsive, empathetic, and effective for every student.

Content Creation and Curation

AI is increasingly playing a significant role in the development and curation of content, changing the way instructional materials are designed, delivered, and customized. By generating quizzes, study guides, course outlines, and more, AI tools are helping educators streamline content development. Having AI tools assist with this work frees up valuable time for higher-level thinking on your part and allows you to focus on engaging directly with students.

Generative AI has the ability to create educational content that is tailored to specific learning goals, student needs, and curriculum standards. The important part is to make sure you tell the tool about your goals, needs, and the standards you need to adhere to. If you've ever thought about creating individualized study materials for multiple sections of a large class, you know that's a near-impossible task for one instructor. With AI, though, generating customized quizzes or study guides becomes a realistic and efficient process. Tools like ChatGPT and other custom GPTs can generate questions on specific topics, adapt the level of difficulty, and provide detailed feedback for students based on their answers. You can ask ChatGPT to create a set of practice questions on photosynthesis. It will generate different types of questions, multiple choice, fill-in-the-blank, or even short-answer questions, and it will automatically provide feedback to responses and offer explanations.

Consider the assistance AI tools can provide as you put together a course outline. If an instructor is taking on a new course on health informatics, a great way to start is to provide a generative AI with key objectives and essential topics and to ask for a course outline to evaluate. Consider the following prompt.

User Prompt: I am teaching a 14-week course titled Introduction to Health Informatics at a public university. Please create a course outline based on the following details. The overall course objectives are:

- Explore the use of computer and emerging technology for the safe delivery of professional nursing practice.
- Assess the effects of emerging health care technologies and their impact within organizational systems on nursing practice and outcomes.
- Evaluate the credibility of sources of information including but not limited to databases and internet resources (in research and evidence-based care).
- Recognize the role of information technology and health literacy in improving patient care outcomes and creating a safe care environment.
- Utilize information technology to support interprofessional communication and collaboration.
- Implement information and communication technologies in health promotion, disease and injury prevention strategies.
- Analyze the ethical and legal issues related to the use of patient care technology.
- Integrate the use of health care technologies and informatics in the provision of quality care to impact individual and population health.

Key topics should include:

- Technology, Security, and Devices
- Safety and Quality of Care
- Telehealth
- Health Literacy
- The Future of Informatics

Include suggested activities or assessments for each topic that are appropriate for students who may already be working in health care, are nontraditional learners, and have diverse backgrounds.

A prompt like the one demonstrated above gives the AI tool enough context to generate a meaningful outline for the course that the instructor could use for inspiration. If you were to input the prompt above into ChatGPT, you would likely receive output like the example below. The full output can be found here: https://chatgpt.com/share/67e3f7af-88bc-8008-89ed-0b37ea6f49e6

ChatGPT:

Week 1: Introduction to Health Informatics

- Overview of health informatics and its relevance in nursing and health care delivery.
- *Activity:* Personal informatics reflection (how tech has impacted their own care delivery or experiences).
- *Assessment:* Introductory discussion post or video blog sharing prior experiences with health care tech.

Week 2: The Evolution of Health Care Technology

- Historical development of technology in health care; key milestones.
- *Activity:* Timeline creation in small groups (using collaborative tools like Padlet or Canva).
- *Assessment:* Short quiz on key developments in health care informatics.

If this were your course, you could now carry on a conversation with ChatGPT as if it was your instructional design assistant, expand the outline where needed, or have it throw out pieces all together.

Finally, let's consider how AI tools can also be used to create an artifact like a study guide from the materials used in class. For instance, imagine a university-level biology course where students have just gone through a complex lecture on cell division. The AI could take that lecture, whether it's a recording transcript or a set of notes, and produce a summarized guide highlighting the key concepts, along with potential review questions.

User Prompt: Create a comprehensive study guide for a lecture on cell division. The guide should focus on key concepts, including mitosis, meiosis, and the primary differences between them. For each process, provide:

- A clear and concise explanation of its purpose and significance in biological systems.
- A detailed summary of each phase, with emphasis on the sequence of events and key cellular structures involved.
- Key terms and definitions relevant to cell division, such as chromatid, centromere, spindle fibers, crossing over, and cytokinesis.

Additionally, include a comparative section outlining at least three fundamental differences between mitosis and meiosis, supported by examples where applicable. Finish the study guide with at least five review questions that vary in complexity. Make sure the guide is well structured and easy to read.

The prompt above would give ChatGPT enough direction to create a meaningful and comprehensive study guide. These study guides can even be customized to fit each student's learning pace and performance. The output demonstrated below is a snippet of the study guide ChatGPT created based on that prompt. The full output can be found here: https://chatgpt.com/share/67e3f18d-8824-8008-93a0-d622c6605bd1

ChatGPT:

Study Guide: Cell Division

Overview

Cell division is the process by which cells reproduce. It is essential for:

- Growth and development.
- Tissue repair.
- Reproduction (both asexual and sexual).

There are two main types of cell division:

1. **Mitosis**—produces two genetically identical cells.
2. **Meiosis**—produces four genetically unique gametes (sperm or egg cells).

1. Mitosis

Purpose and Significance

Mitosis enables organisms to grow, repair damaged tissues, and replace dead cells. It results in *two daughter cells* that are *genetically identical* to the parent cell and each other, with the same number of chromosomes.

Phases of Mitosis

1. **Interphase** (not technically part of mitosis but important prep stage)
   » DNA replication occurs.
   » Chromosomes are not yet visible.
   » The cell grows and prepares for division.
2. **Prophase**
   » Chromatin condenses into visible chromosomes.
   » Each chromosome has two sister chromatids joined at the **centromere**.
   » The **nuclear envelope breaks down**.
   » **Spindle fibers** begin to form from centrosomes.

3. **Metaphase**
    - Chromosomes align along the **metaphase plate** (center of the cell).
    - Spindle fibers attach to centromeres.
4. **Anaphase**
    - Sister chromatids separate and move to opposite poles.
    - Each chromatid is now an individual chromosome.
5. **Telophase**
    - Chromosomes arrive at poles and de-condense.
    - Nuclear envelopes reform around each set of chromosomes.
6. **Cytokinesis**
    - The cytoplasm divides.
    - Two identical daughter cells are formed.

AI-generated content is already being explored in education, though the results are mixed. For example, Khan Academy launched Khanmigo, an AI-powered assistant designed to help generate practice questions and personalized prompts for students. While it holds promise, some educators and researchers have raised concerns about its actual classroom effectiveness, citing uneven results and limitations in adapting to student needs. Similarly, Quizlet uses AI to generate flash cards and study guides based on uploaded materials. These tools can offer convenience, but their accuracy and instructional value still depend heavily on the quality of the source content and the specific context in which they're used.

As these tools continue to evolve, some instructors are experimenting with using AI to generate quiz questions, writing prompts, or reading checks that they can then review and adapt for their students. For example, a faculty member might use Khanmigo to create practice problems aligned with a particular lesson or turn to Quizlet to auto-generate flash cards from a set of lecture notes or slides. In both cases, the instructor still plays the key role of reviewing, revising, and curating the AI-generated materials to keep them aligned with the course goals and student needs. AI's role here is less about replacing the educator and more about streamlining the time-consuming parts of resource creation.

Benefits and Challenges of AI Integration in the Classroom

Think about the last time you introduced a new tool or strategy in your classroom. Maybe it was the use of a new learning management system after your institution switched vendors, or perhaps a tool like Grammarly to help students improve their writing. It probably sparked some excitement at the possibilities, and maybe a bit of frustration as you learned to integrate it. AI is quickly becoming one of those tools that many educators are turning to, not just for administrative tasks but to fundamentally change how we teach and learn for the better. Like any edtech tool, it comes with challenges that demand careful thought and planning.

Benefits

Let's begin with those administrative tasks. AI has the potential to greatly enhance teacher productivity by handling repetitive work that often consumes an educator's time. The main benefit of this technology is its ability to free you from time-intensive, routine tasks that don't require significant intellectual engagement. Think grading summative quizzes or tracking attendance. This allows instructors to shift their focus to higher-order activities, like designing better assessments, mentoring students, and improving overall course outcomes.

On the student side, AI tools like Wolverine Learning Assistant, which I developed as an OpenAI custom GPT, make learning more accessible and adaptive. Integrated into courses, it helps students navigate complex topics by providing practice questions and detailed feedback tailored to their progress. If this were deployed in a philosophy course, for example, it could offer practice on ethical theories, adjusting the difficulty based on how the student responds. A student struggling with utilitarianism might receive additional explanations and examples, while a student excelling in deontology could be challenged with case studies. The aim is to foster personalized engagement that keeps students motivated and consistently challenges them at the right level.

Finally, it can make learning more accessible. AI translation tools like Google Translate help students from different linguistic backgrounds by providing real-time translation, making course material more inclusive. This is especially valuable in settings where students may not have English as their first language. Additionally, AI-powered assistive tools help students with disabilities. Whisper from OpenAI is a speech-to-text technology that allows students with hearing impairments to follow along with lectures in real time by transcribing spoken words into text. Similarly, AI can assist visually impaired students by converting text to speech to describe media or the physical world.

Challenges

While AI brings so many advantages to educators, it's not without its limitations. One of the main challenges is the issue of model inaccuracies. Tools like ChatGPT, Claude, or Gemini can occasionally generate content that is incorrect or misleading. This phenomenon, often referred to as "hallucination," can present serious challenges in classroom settings where accuracy is crucial. This behavior stems from the model's design to provide answers rather than to admit uncertainty. Please refer to Table 1.1 for more detail on this concept. For you, understanding this limitation is essential, as relying on AI-generated content without verification can lead to the dissemination of errors. If a student relies on AI to clarify a complicated concept in a subject like physics, but the AI provides an incorrect explanation, it can lead to confusion or misunderstandings that are going to be difficult to undo.

Another major concern is the ethical implications associated with these systems. AI models are trained on oceans of human-created datasets that include biases. Bias in the training input often leads to bias in the output. Imagine an instructor using an AI tool to generate discussion prompts for a history class on global cultures. If the AI draws from biased training data, it might produce examples that unintentionally perpetuate stereotypes or exclude key perspectives from non-Western societies. If stereotypes are embedded in generated content, it raises the potential of negatively impacting students from marginalized backgrounds. Making the training data for these systems as inclusive and representative as possible remains an ongoing challenge. Some companies have publicly stated commitments to improving data transparency and fairness, but their progress varies. Users can look for model documentation, often called *model cards* or *system cards*, that outline training sources, limitations, and efforts to address bias. For example, OpenAI provides system cards for models like GPT-4o, detailing known limitations and steps taken to mitigate harm. You can review that system card here: https://openai.com/index/gpt-4o-system-card/.

Privacy is another significant consideration. AI tools often require access to student and institutional data to personalize learning experiences, but this raises questions about how that data is used, stored, and protected. Intellectual property issues add another layer of complexity. Something instructors should keep in mind is that student work, once submitted, can be used to train AI systems without explicit consent, raising concerns about ownership and transparency.

Finally, there's the risk of potential misuse by both faculty and students. AI tools that generate content can be abused by students for cheating or by others to spread misinformation. You'll want to set clear guidelines for the ethical use of AI so students understand both the benefits and the potential risks that come with using these technologies in their learning. Similarly, faculty may misuse AI by relying on it to run courses in a way that minimizes their direct interaction with students. An instructor might lean too heavily on AI-generated lectures, discussion prompts, and assessments without tailoring or engaging with the material themselves. Faculty with the know-how might give ChatGPT examples of their writing and use it to directly respond to student queries. This approach will result in diminished learning experiences for students, who benefit from the guidance and interaction that only a dedicated instructor can provide.

In the chapters ahead, we'll explore these benefits and challenges in greater detail, providing practical solutions for those of you looking to integrate AI effectively while mitigating its risks. For now, it's fair to recognize that while AI holds immense promise for enhancing learning, it must be implemented thoughtfully so that it serves all students equitably and responsibly.

I want to emphasize that the purpose of integrating AI into the education space shouldn't necessarily be to give instructors more time for personal pursuits, like getting in an extra round of golf, but rather to create more opportunities for meaningful student engagement. Students value instructor presence and personalized attention. By using this technology to streamline routine tasks, you can invest your time in higher-order tasks like building stronger relationships with students, mentoring them, and helping students develop a better understanding of the material. These outcomes are at the heart of effective teaching.

DISCUSSION AND ACTIVITY

Discussion

As an educator, you've likely already encountered the ways AI is starting to influence teaching, from automating repetitive tasks to creating tailored learning experiences. But beyond the initial excitement lies a need for reflection. How we choose to integrate these tools will shape our workflows and the ethical landscape of education. The questions below are designed to prompt thoughtful consideration of the opportunities and challenges AI brings, helping you align its use with your goals and values as an educator.

1. How do you foresee AI transforming your teaching practices and workflows in the next two years? Consider the tasks that currently take up the most time in your teaching practice. Could AI tools help streamline feedback, track student progress more effectively, or assist in creating something like a lesson plan? Reflect on the areas where you feel AI might reduce administrative burdens and allow you to focus more on student engagement.

Conversely, think about potential challenges. Do you anticipate needing additional training or support to make the most of these tools? Share your vision with colleagues regarding how AI could enhance your work as an educator while addressing any uncertainties you might have about implementation.

2. What concerns would you prioritize when integrating AI into educational workflows you already use? When integrating AI into your teaching practice, ethical considerations are inevitable. Reflect on issues such as bias, privacy, intellectual property, and the fairness of AI-assisted grading. How would you address concerns about AI grading consistency or its inability to fully evaluate creative work, such as essays or critical reflections? And how would you protect student data from being misused or shared without consent? Think about the tools you currently use and identify areas where transparency, inclusivity, and accountability could be improved.

These questions aren't just theoretical; they are meant to help you evaluate how AI fits into your own teaching philosophy and classroom practices. By reflecting on these topics, you can approach AI integration in a way that's both effective and ethical, keeping student needs and learning outcomes at the center of your decisions.

Activity

Exploring Generative AI in Education

This activity is designed to help you take the first step in experimenting with generative AI in a low-stakes and controlled way. Many people feel apprehensive about using these tools, but the best way to understand their potential is to try them out in a safe, exploratory environment. By engaging directly with an AI, you'll gain practical insights into its capabilities, limitations, and how it could fit into your teaching practice.

Instructions

1. **Choose an AI Tool**
   a. Select a free or accessible generative AI tool such as ChatGPT, Claude, or Gemini. Refer to Table 2.1 for more choices and detail. If these are unavailable, use another AI tool that aligns with the functionality described in this chapter.
2. **Craft a Prompt**
   a. Think of a topic or task related to your teaching. Examples include:
      i. Create a study guide for a commonly taught topic.
      ii. Generate discussion questions for a specific reading or lecture.
      iii. Draft a quiz or exam question set for a particular subject area.
   b. Write a clear and concise prompt for the AI tool. For instance:
      i. "Create a study guide for an introductory lesson on photosynthesis. Include key concepts, definitions, and 3–5 review questions."
      ii. "Draft a multiple-choice exam question for an intermediate-level physics course on Newton's Laws of Motion. Include the correct answer and three plausible distractors."
3. **Run the Prompt**
   a. Input your prompt into your chosen AI tool and review the generated output.

Analysis and Reflection

1. **Assess the Output**
   a. Evaluate the content generated by the AI. Consider:
      i. What aspects of the output are well done? Did it provide comprehensive or creative content?
      ii. Are there gaps, inaccuracies, or overly simplistic responses?
      iii. Did the tool offer ideas or formats you might not have thought of on your own?

2. **Classroom Application**
    a. Reflect on how you might use the generated content in your teaching.
        i. Could it serve as a draft to refine and use in class?
        ii. Would it save you time in creating routine materials?
        iii. Are there ways the content could be adapted to better fit your students' needs?
3. **Consider Ethical and Practical Implications**
    a. Identify any biases, inaccuracies, or omissions in the output. Could these issues affect your students' learning or engagement?
    b. Reflect on how using AI-generated content aligns with your teaching philosophy. For example:
        i. Does it support or detract from your role as an instructor?
        ii. Are there ethical considerations, such as overreliance on AI or the potential for student misuse?

This activity is intended to help you overcome any initial hesitation about using generative AI by providing a hands-on, exploratory experience. Reflect on the opportunities these tools provide as well as the challenges they present to better understand how they can enhance your teaching in meaningful and responsible ways.

CHAPTER 2

Mastering Prompt Design

Essential Skills for Crafting Effective AI Prompts

PRINCIPLES OF EFFECTIVE PROMPT WRITING

Introduction

Effective prompts can dramatically enhance the efficiency and effectiveness of your interactions with any AI tool and the output you receive from it. In this chapter, you're going to learn foundational principles of writing effective prompts, designed to optimize your engagements with AI systems. You'll also learn how to identify and sidestep common pitfalls while crafting prompts that truly work in your favor. By the end of this chapter, you will be equipped not only to develop and refine your prompts but also to evaluate the AI's output critically. This will empower you to continuously improve your prompt-writing skills and stay confident in guiding AI interactions toward your desired outcomes.

Clarity and Precision

Clarity, in the context of AI prompting, means presenting a prompt in a way that is easily understood and actionable by the AI. This involves specifying tasks precisely, avoiding ambiguities, and using language that aligns with the AI's processing capabilities.

Precision is key. A well-defined prompt gives the AI a specific direction, allowing it to focus its capabilities effectively. Prompts should avoid ambiguities. Unclear prompts can confuse the AI, leading to outputs that might technically satisfy the requirements but miss the mark on your actual intent. Additionally, clear prompts contribute to efficiency. When the AI understands exactly what is expected from the start, it can often produce the correct or more useful outputs on the first try.

Below, let's look at the components that make up a clear prompt that helps you get the best output.

Components of a Clear Prompt

There are several components involved in the development of a clear prompt. When directing an AI tool, you want to make sure you're not being ambiguous, you're providing consistent details, and the language is clear and understandable. You can even provide illustrative examples. Let's look at each of these.

Unambiguous Task

We don't want to input ambiguous questions or statements when working with an AI tool. It's best to eliminate any uncertainties about your desired output. For example, compare these two prompts:

Vague: Tell me about World War II.
Clearer: Write a 200-word summary of the key events of World War II focusing on European battles.

The second prompt improves on the first by narrowing the content scope (key events, European battles) and specifying the desired format (a 200-word summary). This kind of clarity gives the AI better direction and leads to more focused, useful results.

Consistent Details

To create consistency in your output, make sure that each element of the prompt supports and enhances the overall task cohesively without introducing contradictions that can confuse the reader. Consider a well-crafted prompt:

Example Prompt: Describe a peaceful, sunny afternoon in a bustling city park, with children playing and people walking dogs.

This prompt is effective because it presents a vivid, detailed, and consistent image. This balance helps both the AI and the student visualize and describe a coherent scene.

On the other hand, a prompt like "Describe a quiet city park with lots of noisy children and busy traffic" suffers from poor clarity due to its contradictory descriptions. The request for a "quiet" park directly clashes with the "noisy" children and "busy" traffic, creating confusion. This inconsistency makes it difficult for AI or students to produce a logical and cohesive description because the basic elements of the prompt work against each other.

The key takeaway is to make sure all aspects of a prompt align and support one another to create a clear and unified direction for the response.

Understandable Language

Clear and direct language often works best, as this aligns with what the AI is trained to understand. It can be helpful to think of this like giving instructions to a very knowledgeable but slightly literal-minded assistant. Being specific and using language the AI understands tends to produce better results.

Imagine asking your assistant to visualize energy usage in the United States. Let's compare two ways to phrase this:

Example 1: Make a visual of how energy is divided in the U.S. these days.

This is too vague. Phrases like "divided" and "these days" are open to interpretation. What kind of visual is needed? A pie chart, bar graph, or infographic? Which types of energy should be included? Without more direction, the AI is likely to produce something too broad or off target.

Example 2: Create a pie chart showing the percentage distribution of energy sources used in the United States in 2020.

This is clear! It provides a specific type of visual (pie chart), the topic (energy sources), a location (United States), time frame (2020), and even calls for a focus on percentages.

The more detailed and specific your prompt, the better the AI can understand and fulfill your request as intended.

Illustrative Examples

Sometimes showing is more powerful than telling when it comes to communication. Providing clear examples can lead to better accuracy from your output. Let's consider an example where you find yourself looking for something more creative in the output from an AI tool.

Example 1: Generate a poem in the style of Shakespeare about love, using "thee" and "thou," with four stanzas.

This provides a focused template; it establishes the theme (love), requests a specific style (Shakespearean), includes period-appropriate language ("thee" and "thou"), and even outlines the structure (four stanzas).

Example 2: Write a poem like Shakespeare.

This leaves the AI with a lot of guesswork. What aspect of Shakespeare do we want? A sonnet about betrayal? A comedic scene? What are the mood and subject matter? The lack of detail might lead to a frustratingly wide range of outputs.

The more specific your examples, the better the AI understands the nuances of what you desire. Think of it like giving an artist a reference photo instead of a verbal description.

Why Does Clarity Matter?

Generative AI models are trained on massive amounts of text from books, articles, websites, and code. That means they are especially good at understanding clear, straightforward language, since that is what they have seen most. When you use precise wording and common sentence structures, you are more likely to get accurate, helpful responses. A well-crafted prompt helps the AI focus its knowledge and deliver exactly what you need.

SPECIFICITY AND CONTEXT

By default, AI will give broad and general responses. The more specific and detailed your prompt is, the more useful the AI's response is likely to be. If you're asking the AI to generate text, provide as much context as possible. If you're asking a question, make sure it's clear and unambiguous. Be sure to indicate:

- The desired goal of your content.
- The desired language and tone that are appropriate for your audience.
- The specific format you want for the output.
- The focus of your theme for the content, for example, nutrition, history, analytics, engineering.

AI inferences can be impressive! It's surprising what an advanced Generative AI model can produce in response to a short phrase. That said, when you have a specific goal in mind, it helps to provide specific instructions. Below are examples of prompts of ascending detail aimed at increasingly complex tasks.

Starting Simple

Imagine you're asking a friend a question. You wouldn't dive into complex details right away. You start simple, like asking: "What is cognitive dissonance?"

This is your baseline, the simplest form of a query to get a straightforward answer.

Add a Bit More

Consider tailoring the explanation for a specific audience. For example, if you're explaining cognitive dissonance to high school students, you might say: "Explain cognitive dissonance in terms that a high school psychology class would understand."

This provides a hint about your audience to your AI "friend," aiding in the adjustment of the complexity and style of the explanation. [Adds audience and educational context]

Provide Context

Let's say your job involves helping people make better decisions, and you're curious about how cognitive dissonance plays into this. You might then expand your prompt:

I am a behavioral therapist designing a program for clients struggling with decision-making. Provide an overview of how cognitive dissonance affects decision-making, including strategies for recognizing and resolving conflicting beliefs.

Here, you're giving a lot of extra clues: who you are, who you're helping, and what kind of advice you're looking for. [Adds author, audience, purpose, context]

Get Specific

Finally, if you're creating educational content, you need to be as specific as possible. Imagine you're an instructor designing a course module:

Example: I teach a 300-level online course on behavioral psychology and would like to develop active learning activities for a module on the role of cognitive dissonance in ethical decision-making, emphasizing critical thinking and self-reflection. Using the Transparency in Learning and Teaching (TILT) framework, outline five activities that can be completed asynchronously and five for group meetings of three to five students.

Now, you're not just asking for information; you're asking for structured educational content, specifying the method (TILT framework), the setting (online course), and the type of activities (asynchronous and group). [Adds author, audience, purpose, context, and formatting]

Quick Tip

Complex tasks require detailed prompts, but specificity can be increased and outputs improved using plain language.

Structuring Prompts

Think of prompt writing like giving someone directions, except in this case that someone is an AI tool. It's helpful to think about this in terms of who you are as an author, who will benefit as the audience, and the purpose of what you aim to achieve. Here's how to give those directions clearly:

- **Who You Are (the Author):** This is where you begin. As the author, you're the one guiding the AI. Are you a teacher looking for a fun lesson plan? A small business owner trying to write a catchy ad? Knowing your role helps you set the right tone and focus for your prompt.

If you're an educator, your prompts might focus on creating engaging and informative content that aligns with your lesson objectives and helps students grasp key concepts in a clear and structured manner.

- **Who Needs the Help (the Audience):** This is your destination. This refers to the individuals who will read, view, or otherwise interact with the content generated by the AI. Are you trying to reach kids, experts, or just everyday folks? This will change the type of language you use and how complex the information should be.

  For higher education students in specialized fields, such as engineering or medicine, the content should be detailed and precise. It should utilize field-specific terminology, include references to primary research, and offer deeper insights that enhance understanding of advanced topics.
- **Why They Need Help (the Purpose):** This is the goal of your journey. What do you aim to achieve with the content generated from your prompt? You might want to teach, sell something, make someone laugh, or change someone's mind. Your purpose tells you how to shape the information.

  If the purpose is to inform, the content should be factual, structured, and straightforward to help students understand the material. If it's to engage and inspire, such as in a classroom setting, the content should include relatable examples, interactive elements, and visual aids to capture attention and promote active learning. Additionally, the language and delivery should match the students' level to support clarity and understanding.

Put Into Practice

Imagine you're a biology professor teaching a course on urban ecology. You want your students to understand the impact of city planning on wildlife. Here's how those elements turn into a prompt:

Author: Biology professor
Audience: Undergraduate students in an urban ecology course
Purpose: Have students apply their knowledge and propose concrete solutions
Your prompt might sound like: "Analyze the current design of a local park and identify at least three ways it could be modified to better support native wildlife populations. Use concepts and case studies covered in class to support your proposals. Consider feasibility and potential trade-offs with existing park usage."

How it's been custom tailored for students:

- **Focused on Analysis:** It requires students to use course concepts rather than just do basic research.

- **Real-World Application:** It moves beyond theory, asking for solutions that are practical.
- **Demands Critical Thinking:** Students need to consider trade-offs, demonstrating deeper understanding of urban planning complexities.

By thinking about author, audience, and purpose, you create prompts that get the results you need! This author-audience-purpose framework for prompt design naturally complements the TPACK model I'll introduce in Chapter 3. When crafting prompts, you're balancing technological considerations (how the AI processes your instructions), pedagogical goals (what learning outcomes you want to achieve), and content knowledge (the subject matter expertise that informs your prompts).

TECHNICAL INSIGHTS

Understanding AI Interpretation

Now that you've learned the basics of writing and structuring a prompt for a generative AI, let's look at how these systems interpret and process that prompt. Generative AI models, such as ChatGPT, are sophisticated systems designed to understand and generate humanlike text. These models are built on a specific architecture called the *transformer*, which has advanced the field of artificial intelligence by enabling more efficient and accurate processing of language data. Specifically, this has significant impacts on natural language processing, which we will discuss later. For now, here are the core principles as to how these systems turn your prompts into new content.

Core Principles

Transformers

Transformers are the technology behind generative AI tools like ChatGPT, Gemini, and Claude. These tools all rely on the same core mechanism, processing language by looking at the full context at once. But they each have slightly different strengths. ChatGPT, for example, is great for back-and-forth conversations and creative tasks like summarizing or drafting. Gemini, developed by Google, handles both text and images, making it useful for lessons that blend media. Claude, built by Anthropic, emphasizes safety and steerability, which can be helpful in educational settings where tone and reliability matter. Thanks to transformers, these tools can understand and respond to language more effectively than earlier AI systems.

Before transformers, AI systems read text one word at a time, in order. That might sound fine, but it meant the system struggled to remember what came earlier in a sentence. If the clues it needed to understand something were far apart, it had a tough time putting the pieces together.

Transformers changed that. Instead of reading left to right, they look at all the words in a sentence at once. They use something called "attention," which helps the model focus on the most relevant words in a sentence based on the context. It's like giving the model a highlighter that lights up the key parts that shape meaning. This allows it to weigh which words to pay closest attention to when forming a response.

Let's take a quick example: "After putting on my glasses, I saw the bat flying in the sky."

Older AI models might have stumbled on the word "bat." Is it a flying mammal or sports equipment? They'd only know for sure after reaching "flying in the sky" and might need to backtrack. But a transformer sees the whole sentence at once. It notices "flying in the sky" right away and understands that "bat" refers to the animal.

This big-picture approach helps transformers grasp meaning faster and more accurately. It's one reason why tools that use transformers can write, translate, summarize, and hold conversations so effectively. They're not reading word by word; they're seeing the entire picture.

Tokenization

When you write a prompt and enter it into an AI tool, the model breaks it into small parts called *tokens*. Tokens can be words, parts of words, or even punctuation marks. It's like reading a recipe by looking at the ingredients and steps instead of the whole thing at once. For example, the sentence "I saw a bat" becomes ["I," "saw," "a," "bat"].

Next, the model looks at how these tokens relate to each other to figure out what you mean. It doesn't look at each word on its own. Instead, it uses the surrounding words for context. So, if you write "I saw a bat flying in the sky," the words "flying" and "sky" help the model understand you mean the animal, not the baseball equipment.

Once it understands the context, the model starts predicting the next token. It builds a response by guessing one word at a time based on everything it has seen so far. It's like if you read the first line of a story: "The rain poured down in sheets as the detective stepped out of her car." You might expect a mystery to unfold. The model does something similar, drawing on patterns from everything it has learned.

Putting it together:

- *Tokenization*: "Tell me a joke" becomes ["Tell," "me," "a," "joke"].
- *Understanding Context*: The model figures out you want something funny.
- *Generating a Response*: It predicts a full joke based on what it knows about humor.

Contextual Understanding

After your input has been tokenized, these systems use attention to figure out meaning.

Attention helps the model decide which words in a sentence matter most to each other. It's a bit like being at a noisy party and focusing on just one person's voice. You tune out the background and zero in on the most relevant words. That's what attention does for AI. It highlights the parts of a sentence that give the most context.

Going back to this sentence: "After putting on my glasses, I saw the bat flying in the sky."

The word "bat" is ambiguous. It could mean an animal or a baseball bat. But when the model sees the word "flying," it gives that word more attention because it helps clarify that we're talking about the animal.

Instead of treating all words equally, the model scores how relevant each word is to the others. Words that help explain meaning get higher scores. In this case, "flying" and "sky" would get high scores in relation to "bat," while words like "putting" or "glasses" would get lower scores.

This scoring isn't static. It shifts depending on the sentence. That's one of the transformer's strengths. It can adjust its focus based on the context, making its understanding more accurate and its responses more relevant.

Training and Fine-Tuning

Generative AI models like ChatGPT are incredibly powerful because they undergo extensive training on vast amounts of data. This includes books, articles, websites, and other forms of text. The aim of this training is to help the model learn the nuances of language, grammar, facts, and some level of reasoning. So, just how do these AI companies train their models?

Massive Datasets

Training a generative AI model starts with feeding it a massive amount of text. Since the rise of the internet in the 1990s, people have shared an incredible variety of information online. That content became the raw material for AI learning.

The data used includes everything from classic literature and textbooks to blogs, news articles, discussion forums, and code. Even things like meeting notes, emails, and Wikipedia entries are part of the mix. The goal is to give the model a wide range of voices, styles, and topics so it can understand and respond to all kinds of prompts in a way that feels natural to the person using it.

Preprocess the Data

Before an AI model can be trained, its data needs a good cleaning. Not everything online is useful for teaching a model how to understand and use language well.

Some of it is messy, repetitive, or just plain nonsense. So, the first step is removing anything that could confuse the model.

Think of it like prepping your classroom. You clear off the bulletin board, toss the outdated flyers, and keep only what helps students focus. In AI training, engineers do something similar. They filter out typos, ads, random characters, and content that's offensive or irrelevant.

Consider these examples:

- "The quick brown fox jumps over the lazy dog." (useful)
- "Buy now!!! $$$ CLICK HERE!!!" (not useful)
- "LOL OMG!!! #funny #meme 😂😂😂" (also not useful)
- "In 1492, Columbus sailed the ocean blue." (useful)
- "The theory of relativity explains how space and time are linked." (useful)

What's left after this cleaning process is a dataset filled with clear, helpful text. That way, the AI model can focus on learning how real language works, how sentences flow, how ideas connect, and how meaning is built. And no, you won't have to do this yourself. But understanding the process helps you see how the model you're using was built.

Training the Model

Once the data is cleaned, it's time to train the model. This is like teaching a student how to write. You give it tons of examples, check its work, and help it improve over time.

Let's say you are helping a student learn about cars. You show them a red Ferrari and ask "What's this?" If they guess "Ford," you gently correct them and explain what makes a Ferrari unique. AI training works in a similar way. The model sees a sentence like "The red Ferrari drove . . ." and tries to guess what comes next. Maybe it says "smoothly." But if the correct word is "fast," it gets feedback on the difference. The model then makes small adjustments to get closer to the right answer next time.

This happens millions of times, with massive amounts of text. The model keeps adjusting until it can make good predictions. Just as a student gets better with practice, the AI gets better at understanding how language works.

By the end of training, the model is like a well-read friend who remembers just about everything they've ever seen. That's why it can respond in ways that sound thoughtful and informed. It's pulling from a huge library of experience to guess what comes next.

Fine-Tuning

After the main training phase, AI models can be fine-tuned to get better at specific tasks. This is like giving the model a focused lesson in a particular subject. For example, after a general model learns how language works, it might get additional training on medical texts so it can answer health-related questions more accurately.

Imagine you wanted a chatbot to sound like Shakespeare. You might collect a bunch of his writing and have the model study it. That's the idea behind fine-tuning. But in practice, companies like OpenAI have already done this kind of extra training. Because of the scale and complexity involved, trying to fine-tune a model on your own may not lead to better results.

Instead, try to focus on designing thoughtful prompts. A well-crafted prompt can guide the model's tone or style without needing to retrain anything. Want something in Shakespeare's voice? Just ask for it clearly in your prompt.

ACTIVITY

Prompt Design Challenge

Objective

Consider applying the principles of effective prompt writing to develop prompts that are clear, specific, and aligned with your goals.

Instructions

Before getting started, it's worth revisiting the key principles of prompt writing introduced earlier in this chapter:

- Clarity and Precision
- Unambiguous Tasks
- Consistent Details
- Understandable Language
- Specificity and Context

Scenario Analysis: Below are several scenarios where you need to interact with an AI tool. For each scenario, write a prompt that follows the principles you've learned.

Evaluation and Refinement: After writing each prompt, evaluate it using the following criteria:

- Is the prompt clear and precise?
- Does it avoid ambiguity?
- Are all details consistent?
- Is the language understandable?
- Is the prompt specific and contextual?

Reflect and Improve: Enter your prompts into the generative AI tool of your choosing (e.g., ChatGPT, Copilot, or Gemini). Based on your evaluation, refine each prompt to improve its effectiveness.

Scenarios

Lesson Planning

Scenario: You are preparing a lesson for your 12th-grade U.S. history class about the Civil Rights Movement. You want AI to help draft a brief timeline of key events to use as part of your lesson introduction.

Write your prompt:

Assessment Design

Scenario: You are developing a formative quiz for your introductory psychology course and want AI to generate multiple-choice questions based on your lecture notes.

Write your prompt:

Classroom Discussion Support

Scenario: You teach a literature class and are about to start a unit on dystopian fiction. You want AI to suggest discussion questions that help students think critically about power and control in the novel *1984*.

Write your prompt:

Email Communication

Scenario: You want help drafting a professional yet warm email to students who missed your first week of an online course, offering guidance and next steps to catch up.

Write your prompt:

Creative Writing Activity

Scenario: You are designing a creative writing prompt for your 100-level English class. You want AI to help create a story starter that sparks imagination and encourages descriptive writing.

Write your prompt:

Reflection

Once you've written and refined your prompts, reflect on the following questions:

How did the principles of effective prompt writing influence your prompt creation process?
What challenges did you encounter, and how did you overcome them?
How do you plan to apply these principles in your future interactions with AI as it relates to your career or academics?

Peer Review

If you're working in a group, a class setting, or have a colleague who is interested in AI, exchange prompts and provide constructive feedback on each other's work.

- **Find a Partner:** After you've written your prompts, pair up with another participant.
- **Exchange Prompts:** Trade your set of prompts with your partner.
- **Review Time:** Take about 10 minutes to carefully read through your partner's prompts.
- **Provide Feedback:** For each of your partner's prompts, write down:
    - One thing you really liked about the prompt.
    - One suggestion for how the prompt could be improved.
    - Any questions you have about the prompt.
- **Discuss:** Spend about five minutes talking with your partner about your feedback. Explain your thoughts and listen to your partner's perspective.
- **Revise:** Take a few minutes to update your own prompts based on the feedback you received.
- **Reflect:** Think about how seeing someone else's work and getting feedback changed your understanding of prompt writing.

Bonus Challenge: Prompt Optimization

Below is a poorly written prompt. Rewrite it using the principles you've learned:

Original: Make something about cars that's interesting and fun to read.

What would you change about the prompt, and how would those changes improve the prompt's effectiveness?

Example Prompts

You can compare the prompts you developed to these examples to aid in your reflection.

Lesson Planning Example: Create a short, student-friendly timeline of the key events of the Civil Rights Movement in the United States, suitable for a 12th-grade history class. Include five to seven major events with brief explanations, using clear and accessible language.

Assessment Design Example: Generate five multiple-choice questions with answers based on the following lecture notes from an Intro to Psychology course. Focus on key terms and concepts covered, such as classical conditioning, Pavlov, and stimulus-response. Use language that aligns with college-level comprehension. [Insert lecture notes.]

Classroom Discussion Support Example: Generate five open-ended discussion questions for high school students reading George Orwell's *1984*. The questions should focus on themes of power, surveillance, and control, and be designed to encourage critical thinking and student-led conversation.

Email Communication Example: Draft an email to students who missed the first week of an online undergraduate course. The tone should be welcoming and supportive. Provide a placeholder where I can write a summary of what was covered and how to access missed materials. End by encouraging them to reach out with questions.

CHAPTER 3

Implementing AI in the Classroom

Strategies and Best Practices for Educators and Students

INTRODUCING THE TPACK FRAMEWORK

Introduction

In early 2024, at the University of Michigan-Flint's Critical Issues Conference on Generative AI in Education, I witnessed firsthand the potential to transform teaching with the use of AI. The event culminated with a keynote by Dr. Punya Mishra, associate dean at Arizona State University and codeveloper of the Technological Pedagogical and Content Knowledge (TPACK) framework (Mishra & Koehler, 2006). His presentation reinforced my belief that faculty who integrate AI effectively will have distinct advantages in the coming years, accelerating teaching, learning, and research.

The TPACK framework resonated with me immediately. It wasn't just the model's clarity or how it connected technology with teaching. It was its emphasis on thoughtful integration, positioning technology as an integral component of holistic teaching rather than a superficial addition.

AI is already transforming education in subtle yet powerful ways. This framework provides us with a lens for evaluating and integrating these tools. It reminds us that technology is only one piece of the puzzle. To truly enhance learning, we need to align it with sound teaching strategies and an understanding of the subject matter. This alignment helps make technology a tool for enriching education and improving outcomes, rather than something used simply because it exists.

Overview of the Framework

TPACK is a toolkit for educators who want to integrate technology meaningfully into their classrooms. Think of it as a Venn diagram with three overlapping circles, each representing a key area of expertise:

- *Technological Knowledge (TK)*: Understand how to use digital tools and platforms effectively.

- *Pedagogical Knowledge (PK)*: Know how to design effective teaching strategies that help students learn.
- *Content Knowledge (CK)*: Master the subject matter you're teaching.

At the heart of this diagram, where these circles overlap, is TPACK: the sweet spot where technology, pedagogy, and content knowledge work together to create engaging and effective learning experiences.

Why does it matter? Because education technology isn't about using the latest apps or showing off "cool tools." It's about choosing the right tools to align with your teaching strategies and subject matter. When teachers develop a strong TPACK in their curriculum, they're able to design materials that make abstract concepts more accessible.

This framework serves as a guiding structure for educators to thoughtfully integrate tools like ChatGPT into their classrooms. Does the tool genuinely enhance understanding, or is it merely a technological gimmick? Are you integrating it for the sake of technology, or does it meet a real need? Does it adapt to students' needs, or does it promote passive learning? TPACK helps teachers address these questions and use AI to strengthen educational outcomes rather than dilute or distract from them.

TPACK Components

To understand how AI fits into the TPACK framework, let's examine each component and how they work together.

Technological Knowledge

At its heart, TK helps you effectively use digital tools and platforms. This means being comfortable with various technologies from basic tools like Microsoft Word to complex AI platforms. Since technology evolves rapidly, staying current is essential. You'll need to evaluate which tools meet your specific teaching needs and understand the basics of how they work.

Developing strong technical knowledge doesn't require mastering every available tool, which would be impossible. Instead:

- Start with the tools that are most relevant to your teaching approach.
- Experiment in low-stakes situations.
- Share experiences with colleagues.
- Stay curious through tutorials and workshops.

AI tools perfectly demonstrate how TK evolves with emerging technologies. To use AI effectively, you need to understand what these tools can do, where they excel, and their limitations.

Pedagogical Knowledge

PK focuses on the art and science of teaching—what great teachers do to facilitate learning. It's about understanding how students learn and creating experiences that support their growth through various presentation methods, from lectures to project-based activities.

This knowledge transforms teaching from just delivering information to creating engaging experiences. With strong pedagogical knowledge, you recognize that effective learning requires scaffolding—meaning, breaking complex concepts into manageable steps and connecting them to students' existing knowledge.

PK grows through:

- Reflecting on your teaching practice.
- Learning from colleagues.
- Staying informed about educational trends.
- Gathering student feedback.

When technology enters the picture, PK helps you determine when and how to use tools like AI.

Content Knowledge

CK addresses the "what" of teaching, or your mastery of the subject matter. It encompasses understanding core concepts, advanced knowledge, and contextual applications. With strong content knowledge, you can confidently explain topics, break down complex ideas, and help students understand the "why" behind information.

This knowledge allows you to recognize patterns between concepts, helping students see connections rather than isolated facts. When students ask unexpected questions, your subject expertise enables you to pivot seamlessly.

Content Knowledge doesn't exist in isolation. It's interconnected with TK and PK. Your subject expertise helps identify the best technological tools and informs your teaching strategies. With the emergence of AI, strong CK becomes even more important. It allows you to guide students through the learning process and address issues that arise when they leverage AI in ways you both intend and don't.

How AI Fits Into Teaching With TPACK

Try not to think about these components of the framework separately; they are meant to work together. AI provides a great example of how these intersections can enhance teaching and learning when applied.

TK+PK

Technology intersects with pedagogy when AI tools help teachers adjust their strategies in real time. Instead of waiting for the next test to see where students struggle, you can adjust instruction on the spot.

TK+CK

Technology should serve content, not the other way around. The AI tools you leverage must align with the subject you're teaching rather than being generic add-ons. When you do this effectively, students are exposed to learning experiences that might otherwise be too costly or logistically challenging in a traditional classroom. Taking this approach helps technology reinforce the material in a way that resonates with modern students.

PK+CK

When AI is involved, pedagogy and content knowledge should stay at the forefront of teaching and learning. It might be easy to let an AI tool generate a lesson plan, but a good teacher checks that those lessons still align with their learning objectives and sound teaching strategies. Don't allow these tools to educate students alone; instead, they should be used as scaffolds.

TK+PK+CK

The central intersection of all three TPACK components transforms AI from novelty to educational asset. When technological capabilities align with teaching methods and subject expertise, AI amplifies learning.

In a class using ChatGPT to analyze primary sources, for example, the technology processes documents, your pedagogical approach guides the discussion, and your content expertise helps maintain historical accuracy. This balanced integration prevents technology-driven teaching that might dazzle but fail to improve understanding. When properly aligned, AI becomes invisible. The TPACK framework (see Figure 3.1) illustrates the intersection of technological, pedagogical, and content knowledge required for effective teaching with technology.

BEST PRACTICES FOR USING AI IN THE CLASSROOM

Key Considerations When Selecting AI Tools

When evaluating AI tools for your classroom, keeping these four critical factors in mind can support a successful integration.

Flexibility and Adaptability

Choose tools that adapt to your teaching style, not the reverse. A quality AI tool will:

- Allow you to customize features to match your curriculum.
- Let you integrate your own content as your course evolves.
- Offer an intuitive interface that doesn't require extensive training.
- Support diverse learning styles and accessibility needs with features like screen readers and multiple language options.

The best tools balance sophisticated capabilities with straightforward operation. It's worth considering that both you and your students will need time to familiarize yourselves with these tools, so those that don't require excessive time to master may be more practical for classroom implementation.

Figure 3.1. The TPACK Model.

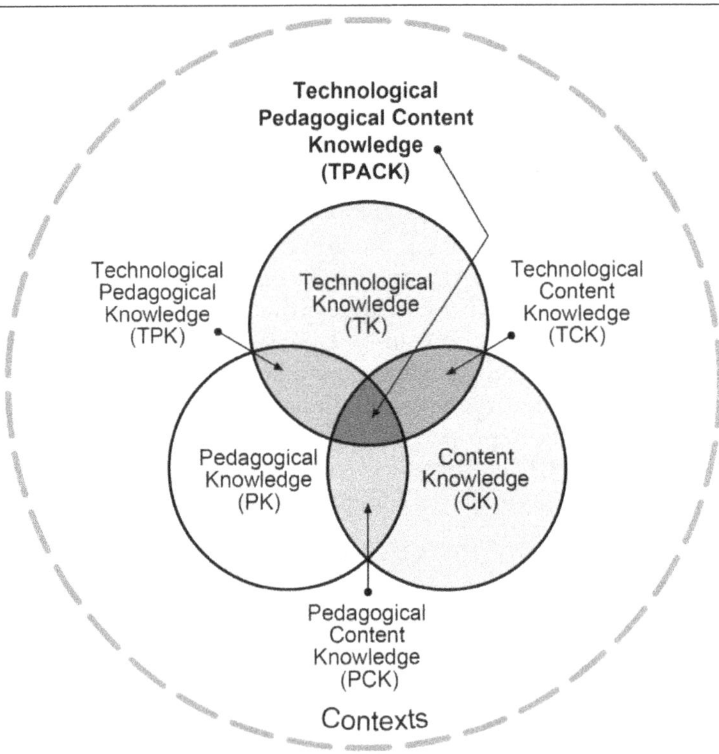

Cost and Affordability

Financial accessibility matters as much as effectiveness. Before adoption:

- Watch for hidden fees or subscription costs that accumulate over time.
- Note that "free" versions often limit the number of prompts or features.
- Check that costs align with student financial realities. Even a $20 monthly fee can exclude many learners.
- Avoid tools that require premium payments for essential functions.

Learning activities designed to work within free tiers whenever possible can help maintain equitable access for all students.

Vendor Reputation and Support

The company behind the tool significantly impacts your experience. Look for:

- A proven track record in educational technology.
- Consistent updates and product improvements.
- An active user community that shares best practices.
- Transparent explanations about how their AI operates.
- Comprehensive support resources including tutorials, FAQs, and responsive help options.

Strong vendor support prevents frustration and lets you focus on teaching rather than troubleshooting technical issues.

Student Privacy and Data Protection

Privacy considerations are best treated as a nonnegotiable priority when evaluating AI tools for classroom use. Evaluate each tool with these questions:

- What specific data does it collect, and why?
- Who can access this data and under what circumstances?
- Does it anonymize or encrypt sensitive information?
- How long does it retain data, and what happens if the tool discontinues?
- Do students have options to control their data?
- Does it comply with Family Educational Rights and Privacy Act (FERPA) or General Data Protection Regulation (GDPR) and your institutional policies?

Tools that require informed consent and provide clear explanations of data usage tend to better protect student privacy and build greater trust in the classroom. A secure digital environment builds student trust and protects their information.

Using TPACK to Evaluate AI Tools

Bringing tools like ChatGPT or Gemini into the classroom is exciting, but choosing the exact tool that works best for you requires more than just picking the latest and greatest tech. TPACK gives us a structured way to evaluate these tools.

Now that we've discussed best practices for selecting AI tools, let's look at how to assess them using the TPACK framework. Starting with Technological Knowledge, we can understand what an AI tool can and cannot do in the classroom.

Technological Knowledge: Assessing the Capabilities and Limitations of AI Tools

Taking time to examine AI's capabilities and limitations before integrating it into your teaching can lead to more effective implementation and realistic expectations. Just because an AI tool shows promise to streamline your grading, generate lesson plans for you, or personalize learning for your students doesn't always mean it will deliver. Ask yourself:

How reliable are its outputs? If you're using a tool for assessment, can you trust that it provides accurate and meaningful insights? Test it on a range of prompts before considering rolling it out to students. Then evaluate whether there are ethical concerns. We've already discussed how bias has worked itself into training data. Could the tool you're thinking about inadvertently reinforce stereotypes? Make sure there are transparency measures in place to mitigate these ethical concerns. Finally, is there ongoing support and training? As I mentioned earlier, AI is evolving every day. It reminds me of the early days of the internet and the dot-com era, when new companies were launching almost daily and the technology was evolving too fast for most people to keep up. The same thing is happening now with AI tools. Will the vendor be around for the long haul and remain relevant? Moreover, will they offer you any training resources, especially for educators?

By carefully evaluating these tools via this viewpoint, you can make informed decisions about whether a tool is actually going to enhance your teaching.

Content Knowledge: Ensuring Tools Align With the Subject Matter and Learning Objectives

It's the intention of educators to make sure the technology we integrate aligns with our instructional goals and enhances students' understanding of the subject we teach. Sometimes we just need to be reminded of that. When considering AI tools in relation to content knowledge specifically, the key question is how well the tool aligns with the subject matter and supports learning objectives without disrupting the academic process.

To help these tools contribute meaningfully to your curriculum, use AI in ways that reinforce, clarify, or extend key concepts rather than dilute them. Meaning, does the tool you selected align with your learning goals for your students? Also consider whether using the tool helps your students explore topics to a greater extent. It really should be an enhancement of subject mastery by aligning with what you're already teaching and helping students make stronger connections to the material. Context-sensitive knowledge delivery means the tool responds in ways that reflect your subject area, offering feedback or explanations that feel specific to the course content. The tool you choose should be able to give subject-specific insights rather than just generic responses. Finally, if an AI tool disrupts the normal learning process in your classroom, requiring too much effort to integrate into your core curriculum, it may not be a good fit. The best AI tools blend into your existing instructional methods without forcing you to overextend yourself.

Pedagogical Knowledge: Choose Tools That Enhance Teaching Strategies and Student Engagement

A well-chosen AI tool should do more than automate tasks; it should actively support and improve learning experiences. When you are evaluating AI tools, the key concern is how AI enhances teaching strategies and student interactions. AI should enhance our pedagogy by fostering engagement, scaffolding support, and offering meaningful assessment strategies. We'll examine assessment strategies more thoroughly in Chapter 5.

AI tools can transform passive learning into an active, interactive experience, increasing student motivation and participation. When used thoughtfully, AI encourages continuous student interaction, reducing passive consumption of information and increasing hands-on involvement. Some of the ways this is done is via tools like conversational AI tutors and gamification elements where platforms like Duolingo or Kahoot use leaderboards, badges, and instant feedback to keep students interested and engaged.

Now, in this context, think of scaffolding learning, in which educators provide support and then gradually remove it as the learner gains independence. AI-driven scaffolding follows the same principles with the added benefit of real-time adaptability. If you are integrating something to help you provide faster feedback, you should ask yourself if the tool is able to provide that feedback in context. So, if you've given a writing assignment and have integrated an AI writing assistant, then it should be able to provide immediate feedback on the structure, coherence, and grammar of the work based on the skills you've taught.

Finally, consider how your tool selection will impact your assessment strategies. With AI capable of acting as a sounding board for students brainstorming ideas, drafting essays, and more, traditional assessments will need rethinking. If an AI can generate a polished response to your prompt, then the assessment may be measuring the tool, not the student. That's why we need to focus more on process, originality, and critical engagement.

As you contemplate integrating any new tool into your pedagogy, you might find it valuable to reflect on these questions:

- Does the new tool enhance interactive learning and student engagement?
- Can AI provide scaffolding support without replacing instructor guidance?
- How will assessment strategies in your course evolve to help students demonstrate genuine understanding and critical thinking?

The process of this type of integration is not a one-time decision; it's continuous and requires ongoing evaluation and adaptation as you learn what works and what doesn't. Regularly seek input from your students and colleagues to fine-tune the role AI is playing in your classroom. By staying flexible and open to iterative improvements, you can better leverage AI while maintaining high standards of learning and integrity.

Making AI a Meaningful Part of Learning

As AI tools transform education, how we use them will determine their ultimate value. In your own process of integration, consider how the tool you've chosen aligns with your teaching goals, engages your students, and, of course, optimizes your instruction. AI-driven activities create opportunities for active learning. Remember that relevance is the key to success. These tools should directly support your course objectives.

Effective AI integration requires preparation for both you as the educator and your students. When you seek out professional development, make sure it focuses on both technical proficiencies and pedagogical strategies. This may not happen in the same space, but make sure you take a well-rounded approach to your development. Teachers need hands-on experience to fully understand the functionality of AI tools. Once you have this foundation, it's more straightforward to learn how to better incorporate it into instruction. All the while, students need guidance on the effective and ethical use of AI in their learning. That could come in the form of a workshop or asynchronous learning experience you guide them toward.

AI IN COURSE DESIGN AND DELIVERY

If you've ever found yourself staring at a blank document, willing a syllabus, lesson plan, or quiz to magically appear, you're not alone. Course design is a mix of creativity and structure. While educators excel at crafting meaningful learning experiences, the process can be time-consuming. Enter AI to act as your assistant. This digital colleague can help you draft materials, organize ideas, and provide scaffolding, allowing you to focus on the parts of teaching that count most.

Designing Courses With AI

AI is now reshaping the way courses are designed by helping instructors efficiently move from blank pages to structured learning experiences. Prompted correctly,

AI can create course outlines based on key learning objectives, generate lesson plans, and identify gaps in your syllabus. Instead of starting from scratch, you can use AI-generated drafts as a foundation, which you can then customize to fit your teaching style and administrative needs. Let's say you're developing an online course on public health. You can prompt AI with:

Generate a 14-week course outline on health care professionalism and leadership. Include key topics, weekly learning objectives for each module, and suggested activities. This is an undergraduate course in a school of public health. Make sure everything created is framed by the following course objectives. [Insert course objectives.]

The result? A structured framework that saves you hours of initial planning. From there, you refine the AI's output to align it with course objectives, program goals, and your personal approach to teaching.

Streamlining Content Creation

AI can also lighten the load when it comes to generating quizzes, discussion prompts, and study materials. This doesn't mean outsourcing all course content to a machine. Rather, it allows you to focus on refining your teaching materials and tailoring them to your students.

Need a structured breakdown of a topic? AI can draft lesson plans by organizing your ideas into logical sequences, providing scaffolding that makes planning more efficient. Need help creating a quiz or assessment? AI can create multiple-choice questions, short-answer prompts, or case study scenarios based on existing course materials. If a topic needs more reinforcement, you can more easily develop additional practice problems or variations of a complex concept. Finally, AI has a knack for summarizing key concepts. So if your students are reading through lengthy articles and materials, and they want to make sure they understand or have an artifact they can quickly reference, AI can generate summaries to highlight critical takeaways and make it easier to understand.

Imagine you've just delivered a lecture on climate policy, and you want to assess student comprehension. Rather than crafting every question yourself, try the following prompt that will require notes from your lecture:

"I teach an undergraduate political science course. Generate five discussion questions based on the key themes of today's lecture on climate change policy. Include both broad and specific questions that encourage critical thinking. These are my notes from the lecture: [Insert lecture notes.]"

If you enter that, or a similar prompt, into ChatGPT, it should quickly provide a solid starting point that you can then refine to better align with your lecture and the depth of discussion you'd like in your classroom.

Tailoring Materials to Diverse Learners

One of the more exciting uses of AI in course design is to make learning more inclusive. Using AI, we can transform traditional resources into formats that accommodate different learning styles, language proficiencies, and accessibility needs.

One of the roles AI can play is to make education more accessible to more learners. It can adapt course materials to different reading levels, so that learners of all levels can grasp the content at an appropriate level. Take a scholarly article, for example. It can be rewritten in plain language for an introductory course or maintain its complexity for a graduate student population. AI also supports multilingual learning by generating translations, making education more accessible for non-native English speakers. Beyond accessibility, AI can enhance engagement through strategies like gamification and interactive learning, in which traditional assignments are transformed into role-playing scenarios or simulations. The idea here is to help immerse students in real-world problem solving.

Consider someone teaching an online course with a high percentage of working adults who are balancing school with their jobs and caregiving responsibilities. Using AI, these students can now:

- Create podcast versions of key readings to listen to while commuting.
- Generate case studies relevant to their professional experiences, making the content more applicable to them.
- Provide summaries and list key takeaways for lengthy materials, allowing them to engage with the core ideas efficiently.

Setting Clear Course Policies on AI

Now that AI is becoming a fixture in the teaching and learning process, establishing clear guidelines on how students can and cannot use these tools helps create a shared understanding of appropriate use. Should AI-generated writing be allowed in assignments? Can students use AI for brainstorming but not final submissions? Rather than being reactive to AI use, take a more proactive approach in the following way:

- Establish whether AI tools can be used for research, drafting, or proofreading, and clarify what crosses the line into academic dishonesty.
- Require students to disclose if and how they used AI in their work, helping to normalize ethical engagement with these tools.
- Rather than banning AI outright, design assignments that require analysis, reflection, and personal engagement. As of this writing, these are the tasks AI struggles to replicate authentically.

This customizable framework helps instructors define appropriate AI use in their courses. Each section can be tailored to align with your specific course objectives, institutional policies, and disciplinary needs.

[Course Name] AI Use Policy

1. *Purpose*: Our course promotes responsible AI use to enhance learning while maintaining academic integrity. (Customize to reflect your stance on AI integration.)
2. *Definitions*: For this course, "AI tools" include applications that generate content, assist analysis, or provide feedback. (Specify relevant tools like ChatGPT, Claude, etc.)
3. *Permitted Uses*: Students may use AI for brainstorming, preliminary outlines, and grammar checks, like a virtual study partner that helps structure thoughts but doesn't complete assignments. (Adjust based on acceptable support levels in your discipline.)
4. *Prohibited Uses*: Using AI to generate complete work or bypass the learning process is not permitted. Instructors should give clear, discipline-specific examples.
5. *Citation Requirements*: Acknowledge AI use in your submissions, citing the tool and extent of its contribution. (Determine citation detail requirements.)
6. *Consequences*: Policy violations may result in disciplinary action per university guidelines. When in doubt, ask before proceeding. (Modify to reflect departmental standards.)
7. *Support Resources*: For guidance on ethical AI use, consult [relevant campus resources]. (Include available support options.)
8. *Updates*: This policy may be revised as AI technologies evolve, with notification of significant changes. (Ensures adaptability as technologies change.)

Delivering Courses With AI

If AI can help design a course, it only makes sense that it can also help deliver it. While course planning benefits from AI's ability to streamline content creation, the real magic happens when these tools enhance student engagement during the actual learning process. This technology gives you an assistant that helps you keep track of where students are struggling but also helps facilitate discussions, provides instant feedback, and encourages participation in ways that traditional methods might not.

One of the biggest challenges in teaching, especially in large lecture settings or online courses, is making sure that students stay engaged. AI can act as a bridge between students and instructors, turning passive listening into active participation. Think of it as having a coteacher whose only job is to track engagement, answer quick questions, and make sure no one is falling behind.

Real-Time Polling and Feedback

Instead of waiting until the end of class for questions—or worse, discovering after an exam that students misunderstood a key concept—you can use polling tools like Poll

Everywhere to provide instant insights into student comprehension. Imagine: You're delivering a lecture on supply and demand, and midway through, you ask students to predict what will happen to gas prices if global production suddenly drops. The software collects their responses in real-time, instantly visualizing trends in understanding. You can then export that data into a spreadsheet you can upload into ChatGPT to give you insights into how to adjust your lectures based on student feedback.

The following prompt could be leveraged for this type of situation:

I teach an economics course. Analyze these student poll responses about gas prices and supply/demand. Help me identify misconceptions and suggest ways to improve my next lecture. Here's the data: [Insert poll data.]

Q&A Chatbots for Instant Clarifications

Students often hesitate to ask questions in real time because they're either shy or worried their question isn't worth interrupting the lecture for. AI-driven chatbots can provide an immediate solution. Integrated into your course platform, these tools allow students to type questions during class.

Say you're teaching an introductory psychology class, and several students ask "Can you clarify the difference between operant and classical conditioning?" Instead of answering the same question five times or waiting until office hours, students can query modern generative AI tools to get clarification immediately. For example, the University of Michigan has a conversational chatbot called UM-GPT that can be integrated directly into Canvas courses for this purpose. If you're interested, consult IT professionals at your institution for acceptable options for course integration.

Students may benefit from AI-friendly discussion prompts that guide their exploration of the technology: "Try asking our AI assistant to explain the key differences between reinforcement and punishment in learning theories. Then bring your insights to our class discussion."

Sparking Discussion With AI-Generated Prompts

Getting students to participate in discussions can sometimes feel like pulling teeth. AI can help by generating thought-provoking questions tailored to the material you've covered. If you're teaching a history course on the Civil Rights Movement, AI can help you develop interesting and engaging discussion questions. Consider the following AI prompt to kick things off:

I'm teaching a unit on the Civil Rights Movement. Generate five discussion questions that will encourage critical thinking and student engagement. The questions should connect historical events to contemporary issues and prompt students to analyze cause and effect. Focus on themes like leadership, grassroots organizing, and social change strategies. Include perspectives from underrepresented voices.

The above prompt could easily be edited to add specific contemporary issues or learning objectives you'd like to explore. AI-generated prompts help keep discussions fresh and inclusive by giving all students the chance to engage, whether they are outspoken or reserved.

Making Information More Accessible

I'm a strong believer that education should be accessible to all students, regardless of their learning preferences or abilities. These AI-powered tools help to bridge that accessibility gap by offering different ways to engage with course content. Whether it's converting text to speech, adding captions, adding real-time captions, or summarizing complex material, AI can make learning more inclusive and adaptable.

Some students absorb information better through listening rather than reading. Text-to-speech tools transform written content into audio, making it easier for auditory learners, students with visual impairments, and those who prefer to multitask. With that in mind, if you find yourself serving one of these populations, consider the following actionable advice:

- Convert written content on Canvas or Blackboard into audio podcasts using tools like Google Notebook LM.
- Experiment with different voices and speeds to find the most effective options for your audience.
- Provide students with both written and audio versions of important readings, so they can choose their preferred method of engagement.

If you were teaching a history course, you might consider uploading your lecture notes into Google's Notebook LM, an AI note-taking application that can transform written content into audio format, allowing you to generate podcast-style recordings for your students. Your students could then listen during their commute or while exercising, making study time more flexible and accessible.

For students who are deaf or hard of hearing, or those who simply process information better when reading, real-time captions are a game-changer. Enabling Zoom captions in hybrid classes helps both in-person and remote students follow the lecture in real time. This helps your students who might miss spoken details due to background noise or hearing difficulties.

AI-driven tools offer multiple avenues for students to engage with course materials based on their personal learning styles. Two key areas where AI can really help are content summarization and multimodal learning.

Dense academic readings can be overwhelming, especially for students with cognitive disabilities, ADHD, or those learning English as a second language. AI-powered summarization tools can help by distilling key points into more digestible formats.

- Provide both the original text and its AI-generated summary, so students can choose the level of detail that works best for them.

- Use AI to generate quick overviews of research articles to help students grasp essential findings before diving into the full readings.

The following prompt, when input with your content, will give you a summary, a table of contents, important points covered, a FAQ, and a knowledge check. The idea here is for you to more quickly generate approachable learning materials based on more complex information that allows you to build a low-stakes assessment for students.

Summary Prompt: I'm going to give you text and files as input; please generate the following outputs: (1) an overall summary of the content, (2) a table of contents based on the important points, (3) a list of important points with a one- or two-sentence summary for each point, (4) a set of frequently asked questions (FAQs) along with answers based on the content, and (5) using the heading Knowledge Check Questions a set of questions for faculty to use as a learning check-in, aimed at assessing student understanding of the content. Use a mix of open-ended, multiple-choice, or true/false questions. Be sure to include the correct answer and a brief explanation and rationale for each question. Be sure that all outputs are concise, accurate, and tailored for academic use, facilitating effective learning and engagement. [Insert or attach content.]

Supporting Instructors With AI

We all know that teaching is more than just delivering content. It often involves endless administrative tasks like navigating committee work, formatting course materials, evaluating new tools to integrate into your course, and responding to student questions. You have the opportunity to lighten this load using AI to focus on higher-level thinking and creating meaningful student interactions.

Reduce Administrative Burden

AI can handle repetitive administrative tasks that consume your time. For example, you could develop templates for common student questions by uploading your syllabus to ChatGPT with a prompt such as this one:

You are a teaching assistant helping manage student communications. Write three to four clear, professional response templates for these common student questions: (1) When are your office hours? (2) What is your late assignment policy? (3) Where can I find the required readings for this course? The tone should be helpful and encouraging while maintaining appropriate instructor-student boundaries.

This approach specifies the questions, sets the tone, and creates customizable templates you can reuse throughout the semester, saving you valuable time.

Content Formatting

Building course content in Canvas or Blackboard can often require HTML knowledge that many instructors lack. AI can generate properly formatted HTML that creates visually appealing, accessible content without manual coding. This converts your content into structured layouts with tables, callout boxes, and organized sections while you focus on course content rather than technical formatting.

You could try using a prompt like this to get started:

I need to create a navigable page in Instructure Canvas with multiple sections. Please write HTML and in-line CSS for a page that includes a clickable table of contents at the top, five distinct content sections with anchor links, clean semantic structure, and inline CSS for consistent styling. Include clear code comments indicating where to customize section titles and content. [Insert course content.]

This prompt specifies exactly what you need: a navigable page with a table of contents, anchor links, proper structure, and styling. It also includes clear markers that make future customization easy.

Requirements Mapping

AI can help align student work with rubric criteria, enhancing grading consistency and efficiency. By analyzing submissions against your rubric, AI identifies alignment points, suggests improvements, and generates specific feedback. This process is useful for any assessment that maps content to established requirements.

Here's a sample prompt you might experiment with:

I have a [assignment type] that needs to be evaluated against a rubric. Here's the rubric criteria: [Insert rubric criteria with point values and expectations.]
Here's the submission: [Insert submission content.] Please analyze this submission against each rubric criterion. For each criterion: Identify specific parts that meet or fail requirements, generate constructive feedback highlighting strengths and areas for improvement, and include specific examples from their work.

This prompt creates structured, consistent feedback that remains personalized to each student's submission while directly tied to your rubric elements.

Product Evaluations

AI can save you hours of research when considering new edtech tools by generating comparative analyses and highlighting key features. Instead of manually reviewing multiple platforms, use AI to gather insights about functionality, integration capabilities, and potential drawbacks.

Consider testing out a prompt such as this one:

I'm evaluating different edtech tools for my asynchronous undergraduate writing course, which emphasizes student collaboration and low-stakes formative feedback. Please generate a table comparing [Tool 1], [Tool 2], and [Tool 3]. Include: Description, Key Features, Strengths, Weaknesses, Integration Options, User Experience, Cost, and Best Use Cases. Base the analysis on real-world user experiences and expert reviews. Summarize key insights below the table, and highlight which tool might best support collaborative learning and efficient feedback workflows in an online environment. [Include other specific teaching needs that apply to your situation.]

This creates a side-by-side comparison with all critical aspects covered, helping you make informed decisions aligned with your pedagogical goals.

AI Assistance for Meetings

AI can streamline committee work by managing agendas, summarizing discussions, and tracking action items. Faculty can often struggle with excessive documentation and follow-up. AI can automate minute-taking, extract key decisions, and maintain continuity between meetings. For accreditation committees, AI can synthesize multiple reports into concise summaries and align findings with institutional standards.

A prompt like this could help illustrate the concept in action:

Generate a structured summary of accreditation committee discussions based on meeting transcripts. [Insert meeting transcript and supporting reports.] Identify key themes, unresolved issues, and areas requiring further review. Align findings with accreditation standards [insert accreditation criteria], highlighting evidence that supports compliance or areas needing improvement. Format the output as a draft report with Executive Summary, Findings, Recommendations and Action Items sections.

This creates an organized, submission-ready draft that captures essential information while significantly reducing faculty workload.

Enhancing the Learning Environment

Now that we've seen how AI helps instructors streamline tasks, let's shift gears and look at how it can directly impact students. Your students don't need to only experience AI behind the scenes. It actively shapes the way students learn, encouraging more engagement, sharper critical thinking, and more personalized feedback. So, how can we make the most of it to create a richer, more dynamic learning environment?

Brainstorming and Idea Generation

One of the easiest ways to elevate classroom discussions and project-based learning is by leveraging AI for brainstorming. AI tools can transform classroom discussions and project-based learning by helping students overcome blank page paralysis. ChatGPT can generate discussion questions or project ideas that expand thinking beyond textbook definitions and jumpstart creativity.

Consider the following simple prompt for a sustainability course: "What are some innovative applications of renewable energy in urban settings?" This prompt will generate ideas like vertical wind turbines on skyscrapers or piezoelectric sidewalks that generate power from footsteps.

For more sophisticated results, try:

Generate a diverse set of project ideas exploring [topic]. Consider technological, social, economic, and environmental angles. For each idea, provide real-world applications and implementation challenges. Focus on solutions developable within [time frame] using available resources. Include both conventional and unconventional approaches and how these ideas might evolve over the next 5–10 years.

This multidimensional prompt helps students develop more sophisticated project proposals by incorporating practical considerations and future trends.

Feedback and Reflection

Good feedback helps students reflect on their work in a way that leads to genuine improvement. AI transforms feedback from delayed comments into an immediate, interactive process. Students can receive instant suggestions rather than waiting days for instructor feedback, enabling them to compare AI insights with course materials and refine their work promptly. This approach helps students better understand their learning process and build independent assessment skills.

A basic prompt like "What could be improved in this essay, and how? [insert essay]" delivers immediate constructive feedback. ChatGPT will identify unclear arguments, offer alternative perspectives, and highlight evidence gaps. While this doesn't replace instructor critique, it creates a dynamic revision cycle that helps students develop critical thinking through incremental improvements.

For a more detailed analysis, consider this prompt:

Review my essay and provide targeted feedback on argument clarity, evidence usage, and logical flow. For each suggestion, explain why it would strengthen the work and provide a specific example of how to implement the improvement. Include questions that prompt deeper analysis of key claims. Focus on sections with highest revision impact. [Insert essay.]

This targeted approach helps students understand what needs improvement, why changes matter, and how to execute them effectively.

Explaining Complex Concepts

Every instructor has faced that moment when a complex concept just isn't clicking for students. AI offers multiple approaches to explain difficult concepts when students struggle with comprehension. Through well-crafted prompts, ChatGPT transforms dense academic material into digestible explanations.

For example, with quantum computing, prompt ChatGPT: "I'm an undergraduate student taking a computer science course. Explain quantum computing in simple terms with everyday analogies." It will respond with relatable comparisons. AI can also tailor explanations to different knowledge levels, providing simpler overviews for beginners and deeper analysis for advanced students.

For immediate access to this functionality, try the Wolverine Learning Assistant, a custom AI tutor I developed that is available 24/7 that clarifies difficult concepts and provides step-by-step explanations: https://chatgpt.com/g/g-jDrNlZoNp-wolverine-learning-assistant.

Customized Study Guides

Students are often overwhelmed by the sheer volume of reading and research they need to synthesize. AI helps them manage overwhelming amounts of reading by condensing lengthy materials into focused study guides. This tool empowers them to control their learning process while developing strategic approaches to absorbing and applying knowledge, particularly valuable during exam preparation when time constraints demand efficiency.

If you're exploring this approach, the following prompt might be a good fit:

> Create a detailed study guide for [insert concept/course material]. Focus on key themes, main arguments, and supporting evidence. Structure it with clear headings for major topics. Include brief summaries of essential quotes or data. Highlight potential exam questions. Keep explanations clear but concise, suitable for quick review. Format using bullet points and subheadings for easy scanning.

This approach requests specific content elements with a clear structure and exam-focused organization, enabling students to access rigorous academic material in a scannable, efficient format.

OVERCOMING IMPLEMENTATION CHALLENGES

So, you've designed your course with AI in mind, integrating tools that personalize learning, streamline feedback, and even spark more engagement from your students. The potential is clear, and the benefits are promising. But let's be honest, implementation is rarely seamless. The challenge is more than about selecting the right tool; it's about making them work in practice.

Instructors might feel overwhelmed by the learning curve, administrators may hesitate due to cost and security concerns, and students, well, they can be unpredictable. Some will embrace AI with enthusiasm, while others will eye it with skepticism, wondering if it's just another overhyped tech fad. And then, of course, there's the ever-present issue of institutional resistance, because if there's one thing education does well, it's sticking to tradition.

The good news? These hurdles aren't insurmountable. In this section, we're going to break down the most common implementation challenges—technical barriers, training gaps, and institutional pushback. More importantly, we'll explore strategies to overcome them.

Let's start by looking at the first major challenge: technological limitations.

Technological Limitations

You've designed an engaging lesson incorporating an AI tool to analyze student writing. You're excited to showcase how generative AI can provide instant feedback, helping students refine their arguments. Then, halfway through class, the Wi-Fi sputters, the AI tool freezes, and what should have been a dynamic session turns into an awkward exercise in troubleshooting. This is the reality of technological limitations in AI implementation, challenges that can frustrate even the most tech-savvy educators. Let's break down the biggest hurdles and strategies to overcome them.

Lack of Infrastructure or Reliable Internet Access

Not all classrooms are created equal when it comes to tech readiness. Older buildings often have spotty Wi-Fi, and even well-equipped campuses can experience connectivity issues, especially when multiple classes are streaming or accessing cloud-based AI tools simultaneously. Off-campus sites, rural schools, and community colleges may face even greater limitations, making it difficult to rely on AI-driven instruction.

So, what's the workaround? A couple of strategies can help mitigate these issues. First, try to have a backup plan in place. Having alternative exercises or non-AI-dependent activities on standby can prevent wasted class time. Additionally, advocating for your institution to prioritize infrastructure upgrades could be beneficial. Investment in stronger networks would help educational institutions better meet the increasing demands of AI-integrated learning environments.

Challenges With Scaling AI Tools to Meet Classroom Needs

A professor piloting an AI tool in their office with a handful of test cases might be thrilled with its speed and accuracy. But scale that tool up to a classroom of 50, or 500, students, and it might not perform as expected. AI systems designed for individual or small-group use often struggle when subjected to larger, simultaneous interactions. Delays in processing, system crashes, or inaccurate outputs can quickly erode confidence in the tool's reliability.

A practical approach to scaling involves stress-testing AI tools before full deployment. Faculty and IT teams should simulate real classroom conditions to identify bottlenecks and limitations. In large lecture settings, like a class of 500 students, relying on a single AI platform may not be feasible. Instead, consider assigning different tools for specific tasks. For example, use one tool for peer feedback on essays, another for generating study guides, and a third for formative quizzes. This approach spreads out the demand and allows instructors to align each tool with a particular learning goal.

High Costs Associated With Implementing Cutting-Edge Technologies

AI tools aren't cheap. While some applications offer free versions, these often come with limited features or restrictions on usage. Advanced AI platforms with robust capabilities can require costly licenses, and multiplying those costs across multiple courses or an entire department quickly becomes prohibitive. It's not uncommon for an instructor to get excited about a particular tool only to find that rolling it out for a full semester would break the department's budget.

To navigate these financial constraints, educators and institutions can benefit from taking a strategic approach. Open-source AI tools like Meta's Llama 3, a large language model developed by Meta that is freely available for research and commercial use, provide one viable alternative. It offers many of the same functionalities as commercial products without the hefty price tag. Some universities are negotiating enterprise-level agreements with AI vendors, securing institution-wide licenses that lower per-user costs. Additionally, grant funding and institutional technology initiatives can help subsidize this kind of integration, particularly when educators can demonstrate clear learning benefits.

Potential Blocking of AI Tools

Imagine prepping a lesson only to find that your go-to AI tool is blocked by the network. If you find yourself in a K–12 setting, understand that you'll likely face strict content filters and security policies that restrict access to certain websites or software. In higher education, such hurdles are less frequent. However, if you're teaching in a K–12 environment, you might face more consistent blocks. Always have a backup plan ready, and coordinate with your IT department to understand what's off-limits ahead of time. Otherwise, you'll find yourself in a situation where your students will need to interact with the AI tool from home and bring the results back to class another time.

Faculty Adoption Challenges: Overcoming Resistance and Stigma

Staff and faculty members are the backbone of schools and universities, bringing decades of expertise, finely honed teaching methods, and a profound connection to their disciplines. So, when a new tool like ChatGPT enters the scene, skepticism is expected. After all, higher education isn't known for rapid shifts. But what fuels this resistance, and how can we navigate it?

I've been asked the question: What do I tell people who refuse to learn about this technology, let alone use it? If you've been asked a similar question, try to remember that AI is not going away. I understand why some faculty would want to refrain from engaging with this technology, and it's within the rights of anyone that would like to take that approach. To those I will say: Remember that the people around you will be using this technology, and you will likely be exposed to its output. Emails that you receive may be AI-edited. Data in your presentation may be crunched by AI. The picture you take might be enhanced by AI before it hits the camera roll on your phone. With all this in mind, you will be in a better position if you are well informed about the impact this will have on your everyday life and classroom.

Pedagogical Skepticism and Fear of Replacement

Many faculty question whether AI truly enhances learning or simply adds technological flash without substance. This skepticism may reflect their experience with previous educational technology fads that promised transformation but failed to deliver. Faculty want evidence that AI improves outcomes without compromising academic rigor.

The concern extends beyond tool effectiveness to professional identity. While current AI cannot replace faculty, educators worry about losing the human elements of teaching, specifically the mentorship, discussions, and interactions that define quality education.

Address these concerns by framing AI as augmentation rather than replacement. Showcase faculty-driven implementations that reduce administrative burdens while preserving instructional quality. The real risk isn't AI replacing faculty but educators who embrace AI outpacing those who don't. Universities are likely to increasingly value those who integrate these tools thoughtfully into teaching and research.

Academic Integrity and Professional Reputation

Faculty worry about both student and personal use of AI. Students might be concerned about bypassing critical thinking processes. A literature professor watching students generate AI essay outlines must question whether students develop independent analytical skills.

For faculty themselves, using AI carries a professional stigma. Professors fear colleagues will view AI use as:

- Cutting corners rather than engaging in rigorous scholarship.
- Prioritizing convenience over intellectual depth.
- Undermining research credibility, especially for peer review and funding.
- Diminishing their expertise or intellectual contribution.

These concerns particularly affect untenured faculty and those in disciplines with more traditional methodologies. A historian using AI to translate ancient texts might worry about being labeled a "tech enthusiast" rather than a serious scholar.

Psychological Barriers and Imposter Syndrome

AI can intensify academia's already prevalent imposter syndrome problem, creating complex psychological barriers to adoption. Many faculty members privately struggle with feeling intellectually inadequate despite their accomplishments, and AI tools can amplify these insecurities in several ways.

Faculty often attribute successful outcomes to AI rather than recognizing their own expertise. A professor who uses AI to help structure a research paper might dismiss positive feedback by thinking, "The AI did the heavy lifting, not me." This external attribution undermines their sense of accomplishment and reinforces feelings of inadequacy.

The perfectionism common in academic culture creates another challenge. AI tools generate polished content that appears "flawless" on first draft, setting unrealistic standards. When professors compare their own messy first drafts to AI-generated content, they may conclude their natural thought processes are inferior rather than recognizing the different nature of human versus machine production.

Using AI also creates uncomfortable questions about intellectual contribution. Faculty may wonder, "If AI helped me develop this argument, is it really mine?" This uncertainty leads many to downplay their achievements or obsessively document exactly what they contributed versus the AI, creating an additional mental burden.

These insecurities manifest in avoidance behaviors. Faculty members who feel technologically inadequate often decline to lead AI integration initiatives, fearing they'll be exposed as incompetent.

Practical Solutions

Overcoming the challenges of using AI in academia starts with reframing the conversation. AI isn't replacing scholarly effort; rather, it's a tool that enhances productivity, much like spellcheck, citation managers, or statistical software. Faculty who use AI strategically aren't cutting corners; they're optimizing their time to focus on the aspects of teaching and research that matter most.

The academic community needs more visible discussions about AI as an asset rather than a threat. Encouraging faculty to share their use cases, building support networks, and fostering a culture where technological adaptation is seen as a strength can help break down these barriers. AI isn't a crutch; when used intentionally it's a catalyst for innovation, and it's time we treat it as such.

Professional Development

In the summer of 2023, I served on the University of Michigan's Generative Artificial Intelligence Advisory Committee, a group representing all U-M campuses dedicated to helping faculty navigate the rapidly emerging landscape of generative AI. It's been one of the most valuable and cherished experiences I've had in my career. One of our tasks was to develop a training strategy that would equip instructors with the knowledge, skills, and ethical understanding necessary to integrate AI into their teaching and research. Faculty were already encountering AI's influence, and we didn't want them scrambling to catch up.

We built our approach on three pillars:

- *Knowledge*—We created resources that provided foundational understanding while aligning with institutional policies. Faculty shouldn't need to wade through contradictory information to determine how AI fits into their courses. We developed a repository of real examples showing meaningful AI integration by educators and students.
- *Skills*—Understanding AI concepts, while valuable, may not be sufficient on its own. Faculty often benefit from hands-on practice to build confidence and competence with these tools. We encouraged departments to offer workshops where instructors could experiment with AI in real-world scenarios like redesigning course materials or adapting assessments. This direct engagement builds technical literacy and confidence.
- *Values*—Ethics must remain central to AI adoption. Our training addressed academic integrity and diversity and equity concerns while creating space for open discussions about responsible use. Clear guidelines helped build trust and reinforced our commitment to academic standards.

From these foundations, we developed seven key workshops:

- *Generative AI Basics*: Introduces fundamentals, common tools, and ethical considerations
- *Prompt Literacy*: Teaches effective prompt engineering for better AI outputs
- *Generative AI in the Classroom*: Focuses on integration strategies while maintaining academic integrity
- *Generative AI in Research*: Explores AI's role in various research methodologies
- *Authentic Assessments*: Helps design assessments that promote critical thinking despite AI availability
- *Equity in Grading*: Examines how AI can reduce bias in assessment
- *Civil Talks*: Develops skills for facilitating productive discussions around AI

These professional development opportunities can support faculty as they integrate AI into their teaching, research, and administrative responsibilities.

Stakeholder Engagement

Integrating AI into the classroom is much more than the nuts and bolts of installing it. You might also want to think about how to navigate different perspectives as they come up. Faculty, students, administrators, and even parents bring different perspectives, concerns, and expectations to the table. Successful implementation means understanding and navigating these human dynamics. Stakeholder engagement and policy development are critical, but ultimately, this is a people management challenge.

One of the best ways to advocate for this technology and promote responsible use is to have open conversations about it. Students, faculty, and administrators need to understand both the benefits and limitations of AI so that its role in education is clear and productive. The best way to do this? Meet people where they are.

Some effective ways to facilitate these discussions include:

- *Campus Orientations*—Introducing AI policies and best practices to new students and faculty helps everyone start with a shared understanding. It also gives parents a chance to voice their perspective, and orientation leaders to address questions.
- *First Day of Class*—Setting AI expectations upfront helps establish clarity on how, or if, AI can be used in coursework.
- *Online Discussion Forums*—A dedicated space in your Learning Management System for students to ask questions and share perspectives on AI use can encourage ongoing engagement.
- *Faculty Events*—Creating informal spaces for faculty to exchange ideas, voice concerns, and discuss the role of AI in their disciplines fosters collaborative growth.

By normalizing AI discussions in these settings, you can clear up misconceptions, support appropriate use of AI tools, and build a culture of transparency.

Institutional Policy Development

When developing policies around AI, it can be helpful to aim for clarity while allowing for flexibility. Since the technology is evolving so quickly, rigid or uniform approaches may not suit the diverse needs of different disciplines and teaching styles. The only universal policy a university should adopt? Don't ban AI entirely.

Instead, this policy should allow individual instructors to determine how AI fits into their courses. Some may choose to integrate it into assignments and discussions, while others may limit its use to keep foundational research, math, and writing skills central to student learning.

A strong AI policy should include:

- *Ethical Guidelines*—Clear expectations for responsible AI use, including citation requirements and academic integrity considerations.
- *Instructor Autonomy*—Faculty should have the authority to define their AI policies while aligning with institutional values.
- *Student Accountability*—Clear communication of expectations can help students understand when and how AI use aligns with academic policies.
- *Ongoing Review*—AI policies should be revisited regularly to adapt to emerging technologies and evolving educational needs.

By taking this approach, institutions can create policies that support both innovation and academic integrity, positioning AI as a tool for enhancement rather than a source of confusion or controversy.

I encourage you to reflect on the ways that AI, when integrated thoughtfully into the classroom, can serve as more than just a tool, becoming a dynamic partner in teaching and learning. Throughout this chapter, we explored best practices, examined challenges, and considered the role of AI within the framework of TPACK, reinforcing that technology alone does not drive effective education.

The framework reminds us that every educational tool, including AI, must be aligned with sound pedagogical strategies and content understanding. It's not enough to introduce AI just for the sake of using new technology. Its integration should enrich learning experiences, support meaningful engagement, and foster critical thinking. As you reflect on your own teaching practice, consider where AI can amplify your strengths as an educator.

DISCUSSION AND ACTIVITY

As we wrap up this chapter on implementing AI in the classroom, it's time to pause and reflect on what we've covered. The ideas and strategies presented are exciting, but they also bring new challenges and questions. AI's role in education is going to reshape the way we teach, learn, and interact in meaningful ways.

Discussion

Balancing Innovation and Pedagogy

Bringing AI into education requires a thoughtful approach, where technology acts as a tool to enhance learning rather than a distraction from it. The TPACK framework reminds us that the best technology integration happens when it supports both sound pedagogy and content knowledge.

While AI can personalize learning, automate assessments, and support content delivery, overreliance on it can dilute the learning experience. You must carefully navigate this balance, leveraging AI to reinforce meaningful interactions rather than replace them. The goal is to make AI a bridge between technology, pedagogy, and content.

Questions to Explore

- How can you confirm that AI tools provide more than just convenience and truly support both pedagogy and content expertise?
- In what ways can AI both support and challenge traditional teaching methods, and how can educators use TPACK to navigate these challenges effectively?
- What strategies can educators use to integrate AI while maintaining academic rigor?

Faculty Empowerment and Continuous Learning

When used effectively, AI shifts learning from passive consumption to active engagement, giving students greater agency over their education. Faculty, too, can leverage AI to gain insights into student needs and personalize instruction accordingly. However, adopting AI tools requires continuous learning and collaboration. It's not "fire and forget."

Professional development is key to building confidence and competence in this space. Institutions should offer structured training, encourage peer collaboration, and provide hands-on opportunities so educators can confidently use this technology in their classrooms. By fostering a culture of ongoing learning and adaptation, faculty can stay ahead of technological advancements and create meaningful learning experiences for their students.

Questions to Explore

- What role should student feedback play in refining AI-enhanced teaching practices, and how can faculty create a feedback loop that leverages this input effectively?
- How can AI be used to create student-centered learning experiences while maintaining faculty oversight and guidance?
- Which professional development strategies do you believe are most effective for building confidence and competence in AI integration, and why?
- How can institutions foster a culture of continuous learning and peer support for AI adoption?

Activity

Purpose

AI tools can be powerful allies in education, but not all tools are created equal. This activity will help you critically assess AI tools using a structured approach based on the TPACK framework. By evaluating a tool's technological reliability, pedagogical impact, and content relevance, you'll develop a clearer understanding of how it fits into your teaching practice.

Task

1. **Choose an AI Tool**
   Select an AI-powered tool to evaluate. This could be a chatbot like ChatGPT, a simulation tool, a learning assistant, an AI search engine like Perplexity, or another relevant tool.
2. **Use This TPACK-Based Checklist**
   Evaluate the tool by considering the following key areas:
   Technological Reliability:
   » Is the tool stable and easy to use?
   » Does it function consistently without major technical issues?
   » Is it accessible across different devices and platforms?
   Pedagogical Impact:
   » Does the tool align with sound teaching practices?
   » Can it support differentiated instruction and various learning styles?
   » How does it enhance student engagement and participation?
   Content Relevance:
   » Does the tool provide accurate and high-quality information?
   » Can it be adapted to different subjects and grade levels?
   » How well does it support deeper learning and critical thinking?
3. **Rate the Tool**
   Assign a score (e.g., 1–5) for each of the categories above. Reflect on how well the tool meets your needs as an educator.
4. **Summarize Strengths and Weaknesses**
   Write a brief summary outlining where the tool excels and where it falls short. Consider any modifications or additional strategies that might improve its effectiveness.

Follow-Up Discussion

- Share your evaluations with colleagues and compare insights.
- Discuss any limitations and brainstorm strategies to mitigate them.
- Suggest ways the tool could be better integrated into your curriculum.

This hands-on evaluation will provide a structured approach for selecting AI tools that truly enhance your teaching. By applying the TPACK framework, you'll develop a practical strategy for assessing whether an AI tool aligns with your technological, pedagogical, and content-related goals.

CHAPTER 4

Ethics, Fairness, and Personalized Learning With AI

Navigating Ethical Challenges and Personalizing Learning Through AI

THE ROLE OF PROMPTS

Introduction

Back in the 1990s, when the internet began to weave its way into our lives, we collectively and often unknowingly started putting everything online. All of it. The good, the bad, and, unfortunately, some of the worst aspects of human thought and behavior. Now, decades later, the internet has become an ocean of information, but it's far from pristine. Generative AI models, which rely on this vast sea of data, have learned from both its brilliance and its biases. As a result, the outputs these systems generate often reflect patterns, trends, and associations embedded in the data, for better or worse.

This chapter explores the ethical challenges that arise when generative AI becomes part of our educational ecosystems. Bias, fairness, inclusivity, privacy, and personalization are the core themes we will address. As educators increasingly rely on AI tools to enhance teaching and learning, the need for critical evaluation has never been greater. How do we make sure that the innovations we embrace do not inadvertently reinforce existing inequalities or erode student trust?

To understand these challenges, we must first acknowledge that bias, whether explicit or implicit, is an inherent part of human cognition. Our brains operate through conscious and unconscious associations, forming patterns that help us process the world efficiently. While explicit bias is often viewed as morally problematic, implicit bias functions automatically and without intent. It's simply how our minds work. However, when generative AI systems learn from human-created data, these unconscious biases can become embedded within the models themselves, leading to outputs that perpetuate unfairness or exclusion.

In education, the stakes are especially high. Biased AI systems can impact everything from grading and admissions to personalized learning pathways, often disadvantaging those who are already underserved. Yet this is not a hopeless scenario. By understanding the roots of bias and taking intentional steps such as developing inclusive prompts and critically evaluating AI tools, we can work toward more equitable and just applications of the technology.

How Prompts Can Introduce Bias

The prompts we write to interact with AI systems also play a role in shaping the outputs these systems generate. Our prompts can inadvertently introduce or reinforce biases, but they also hold the potential to mitigate them when crafted with thought and intention. Understanding this dual role of prompts helps us shape our interactions with AI systems in ways that promote fairness and inclusivity rather than reinforce harmful stereotypes. Ultimately, these systems are tools, robots doing what they're told. It's up to us to guide and correct them through the input we provide.

The way you phrase a prompt significantly influences AI outputs, even when you don't intend to introduce bias. Your word choice, framing, and implicit assumptions can all shape the response.

- **Word Choice and Framing:** Asking about "dangers of ibuprofen" yields different results than asking about "benefits and risks of ibuprofen." The first focuses on negatives, while the second produces a more balanced response.
- **Implicit Assumptions:** Consider a prompt like "How can parents help their children succeed in school?" This phrasing assumes all students have involved parents, which may not reflect the reality for those with guardians, foster care arrangements, or other caregiving situations. A more inclusive version might be "How can families and caregivers support student success?" which acknowledges the variety of home environments students come from.
- **Loaded Terms:** In academic contexts, asking an AI to "identify groundbreaking work by pioneers in engineering" may unintentionally prioritize traditionally recognized, often male, contributors. "Identify recent innovative studies in engineering" removes the historically loaded term.

Even seemingly neutral prompts can produce biased responses due to the following factors:

- **Ambiguity:** When prompts are vague or ambiguous, the AI fills in the gaps based on its training. A request like "Describe a typical family" invites the AI to draw on dominant cultural narratives, which may not reflect the diversity of family structures that exist. A more inclusive alternative would be "Describe different types of families and how they support one another," which encourages a broader, more representative response.
- **Framing Effects:** The way a prompt is worded doesn't just influence the topic; it shapes the tone, focus, and even the scope of an AI's response. For example, a teacher asking "Why are students today so distracted?" sets the

stage for a deficit-focused answer that may blame technology, attention spans, or classroom environments. Reframing that prompt as "What are some factors that influence student focus in today's classrooms?" invites a more nuanced exploration that includes challenges, strategies, environments, and student strengths. It's not just what we ask, it's how we ask it.

- **Contextual Accumulation:** AI systems often consider prior prompts or conversations when generating responses. A series of prompts focusing on negative aspects of a topic can prime the AI to continue emphasizing negativity, even if individual questions seem neutral. For instance, if an educator starts by asking "What are the problems with online learning?" followed by "Why do students disengage in virtual classrooms?" and then later asks "What are some effective online teaching strategies?" the AI might still lean toward a negative framing, focusing more on fixing problems than highlighting what works well. The earlier context lingers and shapes what comes next.

The Concept of Priming

Priming refers to the way preceding input or context influences an AI's response. In the context of interacting with an AI, priming happens when a particular prompt, word choice, or sequence of questions shapes the AI's understanding of the task and subtly alters the response.

This concept is rooted in cognitive science, where priming describes how exposure to certain stimuli can influence a person's subsequent thoughts, behaviors, or decisions. Similarly, in AI systems, priming affects how the model processes and responds to a given prompt based on earlier interactions or framing.

The AI retains context from earlier interactions, causing subsequent responses to align with the tone or focus of previous prompts. A prompt with something like a prior emphasis on negative aspects of urban development may shape future answers toward similar negativity. In addition to that, even neutral-seeming prompts can guide responses based on subtle framing. A prompt that focuses on "leaders who have failed" steers the AI toward negative examples, while asking about "challenges leaders face" invites a more nuanced or balanced perspective. Moreover, specific words or phrases, like "progressive" or "conservative," can prime the AI to generate responses shaped by cultural or ideological trends embedded in its training data. Finally, the tone and complexity of a prompt influence how the AI crafts its response. A casual prompt requesting simplicity leads to basic explanations, while an academic tone encourages more sophisticated analysis.

To reduce unintended priming effects and encourage balanced AI outputs, consider using the following strategies. Provide explicit instructions; if you want a balanced response, don't be afraid to specify that in the prompt itself. From there, experimenting with variations by rephrasing prompts can help you understand how slight changes influence the output. Then consider multiplicity in your prompts, which means asking for diverse examples to broaden the response. There's nothing stopping you from asking for additional perspectives.

Utilizing Prompts to Minimize Bias

Recognizing that even seemingly neutral prompts can carry bias, the next step is to explore how prompts can be utilized intentionally to minimize these biases. Adding explicit instructions to consider diverse perspectives or emphasizing the inclusion of underrepresented groups can nudge the AI toward more equitable outputs. For instance, instead of asking "Write a story about an entrepreneur," you might reframe it to say "Write a story about an entrepreneur from an underrepresented background." That small shift can significantly affect the AI's response. By adopting strategies that prioritize inclusivity and fairness, we can craft prompts that guide AI systems toward producing balanced and representative outputs. Carefully consider the language and structure of the prompt to avoid embedding unintended assumptions or biases.

Be Specific and Unambiguous

Ambiguity in prompts can unintentionally lead to biased responses by leaving room for subjective interpretation. To address this, use precise language that clearly defines the context and scope of the question rather than asking a vague question like "What are the benefits of this policy?" It's more effective to give more specific context, such as "What are the potential benefits and drawbacks of implementing this policy in a rural high school?" Additionally, avoiding overgeneralizations or broad terms helps to minimize stereotyping. Replacing "Why do teenagers always misuse social media?" with "What are some common ways teenagers engage with social media? Include both positive and negative elements" provides a more neutral framework.

Structuring prompts to encourage balanced perspectives is also important; leading questions that imply a "correct" answer should be avoided. Consider the prompt "Why is renewable energy the best solution for combating climate change?" This phrasing implies a predetermined conclusion, that renewable energy is unquestionably the best solution, and may prime the AI for a response that affirms this perspective, potentially ignoring other viable approaches. To create a more balanced prompt, you could ask "What are the strengths and limitations of renewable energy compared to other approaches to combating climate change such as carbon capture or energy efficiency initiatives?" This revised question avoids suggesting a single correct answer and instead invites exploration of multiple perspectives.

By being detailed and explicit, prompts can keep the focus on the core substance of the question rather than allowing the AI to make assumptions, which lets unintended subtext influence responses.

Question Your Assumptions

Every prompt carries the perspective of its creator, making it essential to reflect on and question underlying assumptions to maintain neutrality. This involves considering whether the wording reflects a particular cultural, societal, or personal bias.

Instead of asking "Why are traditional family structures more effective?" it's more neutral to ask "What are the advantages and challenges of various family structures?" Similarly, challenging stereotypes embedded in the framing of questions helps to avoid reinforcing narrow narratives. For example, rather than assuming a singular gendered perspective with a question like "Why are women underrepresented in tech leadership?" you might reframe the prompt as "What systemic and organizational factors influence representation in tech leadership roles?" Actively seeking input from diverse perspectives helps to identify blind spots and unintended biases in prompts. By critically examining your own assumptions, it becomes possible to craft questions that reflect a broader, more inclusive, and equitable perspective.

Counteract Known Biases

Counteracting known biases, whether historical, societal, or algorithmic, is a must for creating equitable prompts. This requires intentionally diversifying examples and perspectives to reflect a wide range of identities, regions, and experiences. A question about influential thinkers in ethics might traditionally focus on Western philosophers like Kant or Mill. To counter this bias, prompts can be reworded to introduce a wider range of perspectives. For example, instead of asking "What are Kant's main contributions to moral philosophy?" you might ask "How do Kantian ethics compare with ethical teachings from Confucian or Indigenous traditions?" or "What are different philosophical perspectives on moral duty from both Western and non-Western thinkers?" These approaches create space for a richer, more inclusive discussion and help students engage with a wider range of voices.

Additionally, addressing known biases head-on by including explicit counterpoints enhances critical thinking. When discussing educational equity, a prompt like "What factors contribute to disparities in standardized test performance, and how can they be mitigated?" directly acknowledges systemic challenges while encouraging the exploration of solutions.

Including Instructions About Diversity or Avoiding Bias

One of the most effective ways to encourage generative AI to produce inclusive and representative outputs is by framing prompts that explicitly request diversity. Without specific guidance, AI models often default to dominant cultural narratives or majoritarian viewpoints. By including instructions that prioritize diverse perspectives, we can help bring underrepresented viewpoints into focus and include them in the output.

A general prompt like "What are common names?" might yield results skewed toward Western names, due to their overrepresentation in the training data. However, reframing the question to "What are common names from different cultures around the world?" explicitly prompts the AI to explore global diversity.

This approach can also be applied to broader tasks or questions. Instead of asking "Describe holiday traditions," a more inclusive prompt would be "Describe holiday traditions from multiple cultures and religions." These small but intentional adjustments in phrasing make a significant difference in shaping outputs that reflect a wide range of experiences and perspectives.

Generative AI relies on statistical patterns in data, which can reflect societal biases. Without clear direction, the model might overrepresent dominant groups or perspectives, inadvertently include harmful stereotypes, or overlook nuances related to minority groups and complex social issues. By adding explicit instructions, you can shape the behavior of the AI to better reflect values of inclusion, equity, and respect. This proactive step helps make the outputs accurate, socially responsible, and considerate of diverse viewpoints.

Instructing AI to Avoid Bias

Bias in AI responses can manifest in various ways, including reinforcing gender stereotypes, displaying racial insensitivity, or offering unequal representation. Providing explicit instructions to avoid bias is a proactive and effective way to counteract these tendencies.

Consider the following example:

Original Prompt: Describe how to succeed in STEM fields.

This prompt might unintentionally result in a response that focuses on one gender or overlooks the unique challenges faced by minority groups. A more inclusive alternative could be:

Bias-Aware Prompt: Describe how anyone can excel in STEM fields, regardless of gender, ethnicity, or socioeconomic background.

By including the clause "regardless of gender, ethnicity, or socioeconomic background," the prompt explicitly directs the AI to provide an answer that is inclusive and considerate of diverse perspectives.

Explicit instructions act as essential guardrails that guide the AI to produce responses aligned with ethical principles that promote fairness.

Practical Techniques for Restructuring Prompts

Adding keywords for balance, such as "methods," "benefits," "diverse perspectives," or "solutions," can encourage the AI to generate more well-rounded responses.

Original: What are the challenges of remote work?
Rephrased: What are the challenges and benefits of remote work for different types of employees?

Invite Exploration of Contexts: Broadening the scope of the response by including phrases like "in various contexts" or "for diverse groups" can lead to more comprehensive outputs.

Original: Why is health care expensive?
Rephrased: How do health care costs vary across countries, and what are ways to make health care more affordable for diverse groups?

Highlighting Equity or Fairness: You might consider addressing fairness directly by asking the AI to consider equity in its response.

Original: What makes hiring in tech competitive?
Rephrased: What are the barriers to equitable hiring in tech, and how can companies create inclusive opportunities?

Turning Problems Into Opportunities: Challenges can be reframed as opportunities for growth or improvement.

Original: Why are STEM fields underrepresented by minorities?
Rephrased: What initiatives can help increase diversity and representation in STEM fields?

Limitations and Continuous Improvement

Even with explicit instructions, generative AI may still produce biased or incomplete responses due to the limitations of its training data. It's important to recognize these constraints and take proactive steps to maintain the quality of AI outputs:

- It's a good idea to periodically check the AI's outputs for unintended biases. This might include taking a closer look at the content to spot any stereotypes, omissions, or overgeneralizations.
- Consider offering feedback to help improve future iterations of the model. Many AI platforms include options for reporting biased or inaccurate outputs, which can support ongoing system improvements.
- It can be helpful to pair AI outputs with human judgment, especially in sensitive contexts. While AI can offer valuable insights, human oversight helps address nuanced and context-specific considerations appropriately. For example, if you're using AI to help draft feedback for a struggling student, it's important to review and adapt the output so the tone is supportive and the guidance fits the student's individual circumstances.

The Importance of Diversity of Example Prompts

Examples provided in your prompt act as guideposts, shaping the AI's understanding of patterns or themes to replicate in its response. However, if the examples given are limited or skewed toward a particular group, field, or perspective, the AI may produce outputs that reflect the same limitations, potentially excluding diverse or underrepresented viewpoints.

For instance:

Limited Example Set: Nelson Mandela, Mother Teresa.

These examples might lead the AI to prioritize historical figures or individuals associated with social justice and humanitarian work.

Diverse Example Set: Nelson Mandela, Malala Yousafzai, Stephen Hawking.

This broader set of examples signals the AI to include individuals from different fields (politics, activism, science) and diverse demographic backgrounds (different genders, ages, and cultures).

Best Practices for Using Diverse Examples

- **Cover Multiple Fields and Domains:** Including examples from a range of industries, disciplines, or areas of expertise can help broaden the AI's perspective and reduce the risk of overrepresenting any single field.
- **Highlight Different Demographics:** Consider representing a variety of genders, ethnicities, ages, and cultural backgrounds. Including a range of demographics can support inclusivity and offer alternatives to dominant narratives.
- **Include Contemporary and Historical Figures:** Balancing historical icons with modern influencers helps to capture a broader range of time periods and demonstrates evolution across fields.
- **Focus on Diverse Geographic Locations:** Bringing in examples from different regions can help highlight global contributions and reduce the chance of regional bias.
- **Avoid Stereotypes:** Choose examples that challenge traditional or stereotypical associations, demonstrating diverse roles and achievements.

Inclusive Language Principles

When interacting with these systems, applying inclusive language principles enhances the ethical and equitable use of the technology. As users, our language and prompts can either perpetuate these biases or work to counteract them.

Gender-Neutral Language

Generative AI may reproduce gender biases found in its training data. If you ask the model to describe a "nurse" or "CEO," it might default to stereotypical gender associations. To encourage neutrality in outputs:

- Crafting prompts with gender-neutral terms tends to encourage more inclusive AI responses. Even prompts that seem neutral can lead to biased responses. For example, asking "Describe the leadership style of a successful CEO" might return a response that assumes the CEO is male, depending on the training data. Rephrasing as "What leadership qualities are common among successful CEOs?" helps steer the AI toward a broader, more inclusive response.
- Inclusive pronouns such as "they" can be helpful when discussing hypothetical individuals, as this approach avoids reinforcing binary gender norms.

Avoiding Stereotypes

AI can unintentionally reinforce stereotypes embedded in historical data. To mitigate this, you should be intentional with language in your prompts:

- When writing prompts, think about how you can avoid presupposed stereotypes. Even seemingly neutral prompts can result in biased outputs because the model draws on patterns in the data it was trained on. For example, a prompt like "Describe a teacher" might lead the AI to assume the teacher is a woman or fits a particular cultural image. To reduce the likelihood of stereotypical responses, try something more specific, such as "Describe the qualities of an effective middle school science teacher working in an urban district." This added context helps steer the AI toward a more accurate and inclusive output.
- Encourage responses that highlight diversity by setting clear, inclusive parameters. For example, instead of asking "Describe a typical school staff member," try "Describe how teachers from different cultural and linguistic backgrounds might bring varied strengths to a multilingual classroom." This kind of prompt not only guides the AI toward representing diversity, but it also keeps the response grounded in an educational setting.

Respectful Ethnic and Cultural References

Generative AI should reflect cultural accuracy and sensitivity. To achieve this, consider the following guidelines:

- You can phrase queries or instructions to reflect modern, respectful terminology. Don't ask "What are Native Americans like?" Reframe the prompt to "Can you explain the cultural contributions of the Navajo Nation?"

- Think about how you can include context to discourage oversimplification or stereotyping in responses. Adding specific details or historical background helps the AI produce more accurate and well-informed output.

Disability-Respectful Language

AI interactions can unintentionally frame disabilities in limiting ways. To align with inclusive principles:

- Prompts that emphasize individuality rather than defining people by their disabilities tend to generate more respectful and accurate responses. An example of this might be "Describe the contributions of a person with autism in the workplace" rather than "What can autistic people do at work?"
- It may be beneficial to use language that avoids suggesting pity or inadequacy. Instead, promote dignity and focus on abilities and achievements, guiding the AI to produce responses that respect and empower individuals with disabilities.

Incorporating Diverse Perspectives

By incorporating targeted strategies, you can critically evaluate AI-generated content and refine prompts to guide systems toward more equitable outcomes. An educator using AI to generate lesson plans might notice that examples provided by the system predominantly reference Western figures or concepts. By identifying this bias, you can refine prompts to explicitly request diverse examples. A philosophy instructor developing a lesson plan using AI could include something along the lines of "Include figures from non-Western cultures or traditions relevant to the subject matter" while prompting the tool.

Once a prompt has been developed, test it to uncover any biases in the AI's responses. This process includes several steps:

- **Initial Testing:** Try generating a range of responses using the prompt. Reviewing these outputs can help reveal patterns, such as repeated biases, demographic favoritism, or missing perspectives.
- **Identifying Patterns:** If biases are detected, try to identify their root cause. Is the problem with the prompt itself, or does it stem from the AI model's training data? This analysis helps to determine the appropriate course of action.
- **Refinement:** Tweaking the wording of prompts can help promote greater neutrality and inclusivity. For example:
  - » Replace "Write about the strengths of leaders" with "Discuss the characteristics of effective leadership."
  - » Experimenting with alternate wording can offer insight into how phrasing affects the neutrality and consistency of responses.

- **Retesting:** After refinement, repeat the testing process to confirm that changes have successfully mitigated biases without introducing new issues.

By combining testing, analysis, and iterative refinement, you can create prompts that align with principles of fairness and inclusivity while guiding the AI to generate high-quality, unbiased outputs.

Broader Considerations

These techniques are most effective when integrated into a broader strategy for ethical AI use. This involves transparency in how biases are identified and addressed, ongoing education about bias for those interacting with the AI, and periodic evaluations of both manual and automated processes to adapt to evolving societal standards.

Privacy Concerns

In an age where digital tools effortlessly enhance our lives, it's easy to forget that convenience often comes with a hidden cost. For educators embracing AI-driven technologies in the classroom, one of the most critical and least acknowledged costs is data privacy. As seamless and responsive as generative AI tools may seem, they are built on a foundation of user interactions, and those interactions are often repurposed to fuel the application we are using. If we aren't paying for these tools with our wallets, we're paying for them with something just as valuable: our personal and professional data.

When You're Not the Customer, You're the Product

Many AI platforms, from virtual tutors to writing assistants, offer seemingly "free" services to educators and students, but there's an invisible cost: our data. Generative AI requires constant data to improve, and this data increasingly comes from educational interactions.

Every student's query about calculus or writing feedback becomes potential training material for the next model. This creates a feedback loop where private exchanges are analyzed and embedded into AI learning processes. While this might seem like a reasonable trade-off for technological progress, it raises serious questions about the ethics of educational institutions inadvertently contributing sensitive information to tech companies.

This mirrors our broader digital behavior, characterized by a tendency to accept terms and conditions without scrutiny. We frequently share our locations, browsing histories, and voice recordings in exchange for simple conveniences like directions or weather forecasts. Educational institutions often adopt AI solutions without fully examining their privacy implications, seduced by promises of faster grading, personalized tutoring, or automated feedback.

These trade-offs aren't trivial. With each interaction, we offer private data to companies whose primary objective isn't education but profit. These businesses seek to monetize their technological advantage, often by selling data access or using it to refine proprietary systems that generate further revenue. The convenience we gain comes at a cost to privacy that deserves much more careful consideration.

Transparency and Consent

Many generative AI systems operate as "black boxes," meaning that their processes are not fully understood even by developers. This lack of transparency complicates the ability of students, parents, and educators to give informed consent about data usage. Questions like "What data is being collected?" and "How is it being used?" are often left unanswered. Without clear and accessible explanations, it becomes nearly impossible for users to make educated decisions about whether and how to engage with these tools.

This opacity erodes trust and creates a significant barrier to accountability. An AI system might analyze a student's learning patterns, but if neither the educator nor the student understands the extent of this analysis, how can they verify its accuracy or how it's influencing product development? Transparency is not just about openness; it is a prerequisite for trust, particularly when personal and educational data are involved. Institutions must demand clarity from AI vendors and prioritize tools that allow for informed and consensual use of data.

Mitigating Privacy Concerns

Educational institutions face a growing responsibility to protect student data as AI tools become more embedded in teaching and learning. While institutional policies play a central role, individual educators can help uphold privacy standards in everyday practice. Below are four key strategies for mitigating privacy risks, along with concrete ways faculty can participate.

Minimize Data Collection

Try to focus on collecting only the information needed for instruction, assessment, or feedback. When using public-facing AI tools, it's best to steer clear of uploading sensitive or personally identifiable data. This includes any data covered under the Family Educational Rights and Privacy Act (FERPA) or the Health Insurance Portability and Accountability Act (HIPAA). Educators should routinely review materials before submitting them to AI tools and remove names, student ID numbers, or any content that could identify a student. When in doubt, leave it out.

Maintain Transparency With Students

Students deserve to know when AI tools are being used in their learning environment and how their data might be involved. Faculty can support transparency by including brief explanations in syllabi, assignment instructions, or class discussions. For example, if an AI system is used to provide feedback on writing, explain how the tool works, what data it processes, and whether the content is stored. A few sentences at the start of the semester can help clarify expectations and build trust.

Use Secure, Institution-Approved Tools

AI tools used in coursework should meet your institution's data privacy and security standards. Public or consumer-grade AI platforms may not offer the protections required under FERPA or HIPAA. Faculty can help by sticking to AI applications that have been reviewed and licensed by the university. If you're unsure about a particular tool, reach out to your academic technology or IT department before introducing it to students.

Stay Informed About Evolving Policies

Privacy laws and institutional guidelines are regularly updated. While instructors are not expected to be legal experts, staying aware of changes to FERPA, HIPAA, or local policies is important. Many institutions offer short workshops, newsletters, or briefings to help faculty stay current. A quick check-in once a semester can go a long way in keeping your course aligned with legal and ethical standards.

A Quiet Crisis

Data privacy is an issue that doesn't grab headlines, but it should. Educators need to ask hard questions: What safeguards are in place to protect student data? Who owns the information that's fed into these models? And most importantly, how do we make sure that convenience doesn't come at the expense of ethical responsibility?

UNDERSTANDING BIAS IN AI

Types of Bias

The biases present in our society, as well as those detailed in this chapter, are not isolated from one another. Instead, they are deeply interconnected, often influencing and compounding each other in ways that lead to complex and harmful outcomes. For example, selection and stereotyping bias can coalesce in a single scenario. An AI hiring tool trained predominantly on data from male candidates will not only overlook qualified female candidates due to selection bias but also reinforce stereotypes about gender roles in the workplace, amplifying the disparities they cause. To effectively address these issues, we need to examine each type of bias individually while also considering their interactions and cumulative effects.

Table 4.1 provides examples of common bias types, and how they can impact the performance of AI systems in educational settings. While this list is not exhaustive, it provides a foundation for understanding how these biases come up and the potential consequences they can have.

Table 4.1. Common Types of Bias in AI Systems

Bias Type	Description	Example
Selection	Occurs when the data used to train an AI system does not accurately represent the reality it is intended to model. This can result from incomplete data, biased sampling methods, or other factors that skew the dataset. Selection bias can lead to AI systems making inaccurate or unfair decisions.	An AI system trained on data from predominantly high-achieving students in advanced placement courses may struggle to identify and support students in remedial or alternative education programs. This lack of inclusivity risks perpetuating inequities, particularly for students who require additional resources to succeed.
Confirmation	Arises when an AI system disproportionately relies on preexisting beliefs or trends embedded in the data. Instead of identifying new patterns or offering novel insights, the system reinforces existing biases. This can hinder decision-making by preventing the discovery of alternative perspectives or solutions.	An AI model used for recommending educational resources trained predominantly on data from high-performing urban schools might overlook the needs of students in rural or underfunded schools, thereby perpetuating educational disparities.
Measurement	Happens when the data collected doesn't match what we're trying to measure. This creates a misleading picture and misses key factors that are crucial for accurate insights.	If a system is supposed to predict student success in an online course but only looks at data from students who completed the course, it overlooks those who dropped out. This excludes factors like lack of internet access, poor time management, or feelings of isolation, missing the real barriers to student success.

(*continued*)

Table 4.1. *(continued)*

Bias Type	Description	Example
Stereotyping	Takes place when an AI system reinforces or amplifies harmful stereotypes. These biases not only perpetuate societal stereotypes but can also lead to exclusion or marginalization in critical areas like health care access or workplace dynamics.	A facial recognition system might struggle to identify people of color accurately due to underrepresentation in its training data, leading to misidentifications in security systems. Similarly, a language translation tool might default to associating male pronouns with roles like "doctor" and female pronouns with "nurse."
Out-Group Homogeneity	Occurs when an AI system struggles to differentiate between individuals who are not part of the majority group in the training data. This results in misclassifications or inaccuracies when dealing with minority groups, perpetuating systemic exclusion and inequity in high-stakes scenarios.	An AI system trained on limited cultural data might treat members of a particular ethnic group as if they are all the same, failing to account for important differences in language, behavior, or preferences. For example, an educational chatbot designed to support multilingual students might assume all Spanish-speaking learners have the same regional vocabulary or learning needs, overlooking distinctions among students from Mexico, Spain, and the Caribbean. This flattening of diversity within a group is a key example of out-group homogeneity and can result in one-size-fits-all recommendations that feel irrelevant or alienating to students.

When these biases intersect, they can lead to compounding inequities. These are situations where existing disparities are amplified by the way AI systems are designed or deployed. For example, if an AI tool trained primarily on data from on-campus students is used to support online learners, it may recommend resources or support strategies that are irrelevant or less accessible to them. This mismatch does not just reflect selection bias; it compounds educational inequities by reinforcing systems that already overlook nontraditional or marginalized student populations. These are not theoretical concerns. Biased algorithms in hiring, health care, and criminal justice disproportionately harm marginalized communities.

Understanding Bias in AI

At the heart of every generative AI system lies its training data, massive repositories of text, images, and other content that teach the AI how to interpret and generate new information. The training process, while innovative, is inherently shaped by the quality and nature of this data. Bias in AI often begins here.

These initial datasets frequently reflect the biases of the societies and systems from which they are drawn. Datasets may overrepresent perspectives from certain demographics or regions while underrepresenting others, leading to skewed outputs. Next in the process comes how algorithms learn patterns from this data, including undesirable ones. If biased language or stereotypes are prevalent in the dataset, the AI may perpetuate these biases in its responses. Over time, AI systems can reinforce their own biases. Feedback loops, where the AI's outputs are used as new training data, can amplify existing disparities, embedding them deeper into the system.

Who Gets Left Behind?

Biased AI systems can and do exacerbate existing inequities. From there, we should consider the question of who gets left behind.

There's always the possibility that an adaptive learning platform may underperform for students from underrepresented backgrounds. AI tools used for grading essays or assignments might penalize nonstandard English, such as African American Vernacular English, or cultural expressions, like idioms or references specific to Indigenous or immigrant communities, that deviate from the dataset's norms. In my own experience, I've found that generative AI tools seem to favor Western-style writing, such as linear structures, direct argumentation, and explicit thesis statements. These preferences can disadvantage students whose cultural traditions emphasize storytelling, circular narratives, or indirect forms of communication. As discussed in Chapter 1, generative AI often produces inconsistent grading results, varying each time the same essay is evaluated. This variability, combined with the risk of penalizing diverse linguistic styles, underscores why generative AI alone should not be used for grading. AI systems frequently prioritize mainstream accessibility standards, such as compliance with Web Content Accessibility Guidelines (WCAG) or screen reader compatibility, which can fail to address the needs of students with disabilities like those requiring real-time captioning for lectures or alternative input methods for motor impairments. Text-to-speech tools might not support specialized academic language, or adaptive learning platforms may lack features for students with visual impairments. For these reasons and others, it's helpful to combine AI-generated outputs with your own judgment when bringing a new tool into your teaching. Doing so can support fairness and reliability in how the tool is used. Instructor judgment is crucial to account for cultural nuances, assess creative and critical thinking, and address gaps in accessibility that AI tools may overlook.

Real-World Consequences of Biased AI Systems

In an era where artificial intelligence increasingly influences critical decisions, the consequences of biased AI systems have become alarmingly evident. From algorithms determining who gets a loan to facial recognition software misidentifying individuals, the real-world impact of these biases extends far beyond theoretical concerns. These flawed systems can perpetuate discrimination, marginalize vulnerable populations, and undermine the trust society puts into the technology we use every day. Consider the following real-world examples that have disrupted lives, exacerbated inequities, and challenged ethical standards.

Facial Recognition Errors

Facial recognition systems have been shown to misidentify individuals from certain ethnic groups at alarming rates, largely due to underrepresentation in training datasets. Joy Buolamwini and Gebru's groundbreaking study at the Massachusetts Institute of Technology exposed how leading facial recognition technologies performed significantly worse when analyzing individuals with darker skin tones and women. The study revealed that error rates for identifying darker-skinned women were as high as 34.7%, compared to near-perfect accuracy for lighter-skinned men (Hardesty, 2018). These inaccuracies don't just create occasional inconveniences; they can have life-altering consequences. Wrongful arrests stemming from misidentifications damage reputations and erode trust in law enforcement and lead to unjust surveillance of minority communities (Hardesty, 2018). Additionally, these systems perpetuate institutional biases by disproportionately targeting marginalized communities, further entrenching systemic inequities. These findings highlight how biased training data leads to systemic failures.

Beyond policing, the same flawed algorithms can reinforce discrimination in areas like employment verification or access to essential services. Buolamwini and Gebru's work serves as a call to action, emphasizing the need for more diverse datasets, stricter evaluation protocols, and accountability mechanisms to prevent these tools from perpetuating societal inequities.

Bias in Predictive Policing

Building on the issues identified with facial recognition errors, predictive policing systems demonstrate another alarming example of biased AI systems in action. These tools analyze historical crime data to predict where crimes are likely to occur in the future. However, bias inherent in historic crime data can cause AI systems to disproportionately target certain neighborhoods or demographic groups, leading to overpolicing and reinforcing systemic inequities. Much like the pre-crime technology portrayed in the 2002 movie *Minority Report*, these systems aim to anticipate criminal activity but often exacerbate existing societal biases instead of neutralizing them.

ProPublica's widely cited investigation into predictive policing exposed significant issues with the COMPAS model (Correctional Offender Management Profiling for Alternative Sanctions). This tool, used across the United States in pretrial court assessments, was found to incorrectly identify white defendants as low risk 23.5% of the time while misclassifying Black defendants as high risk 44.9% of the time (Angwin et al., 2016). Such discrepancies have profound consequences: Black defendants are more likely to face harsher sentencing recommendations and endure stigmatization that can affect housing, employment, and community reintegration opportunities. Meanwhile, the overpolicing of specific neighborhoods based on flawed predictions leads to a cycle where these areas continue to be disproportionately monitored, regardless of the actual rates of crime.

ProPublica's investigation makes it clear that we must fundamentally rethink how predictive policing systems are designed and used. Addressing bias requires not just surface-level adjustments but a thorough overhaul of training datasets to root out embedded prejudices. Without these changes, predictive models will continue to reinforce the inequities they were intended to mitigate.

These same predictive techniques are increasingly showing up in education. Early warning systems, for example, are used to flag students at risk of dropping out or falling behind. While these tools are well intentioned, they are often built on data that reflect structural inequities, such as attendance patterns, disciplinary records, or GPA. These indicators are frequently taken at face value without considering the broader context. As a result, students from historically marginalized backgrounds may be disproportionately labeled as high risk. This reinforces deficit-based narratives and can limit the kinds of opportunities and support made available to them. Just as in predictive policing, biased data in education can quietly shape who gets help, who is monitored more closely, and who is overlooked.

Gender Bias in Language Models

Given their foundation in massive structured and unstructured datasets stemming from the real world, language models inherently reflect and often magnify the societal biases present in the text they learn from. Generative AI systems might do something like produce gender-biased outputs by disproportionately associating caregiving professions like "nurse" and "teacher" with women while linking leadership roles such as "CEO" and "engineer" with men. Beyond the output of LLMs, consider what might happen when a gender-biased AI tool is used to generate job suggestions based on an analysis of their résumé. A woman with a background in general management may consistently receive recommendations for HR or administrative positions, while a man with a similar résumé might be directed toward leadership or executive roles. Such outputs reinforce narrow views of gender roles, influencing perceptions and decision-making processes across industries.

The biases in language models extend beyond professions to emotional characteristics and behaviors. As highlighted by the *MIT News*, large language models may disproportionately associate emotions like "anxious," "depressed," and "devastated" with femininity, ignoring the reality that individuals of all genders experience these emotions (Gordon, 2023). Similarly, traditionally "masculine" attributes such as "assertive," "confident," and "logical" are often overrepresented in association with men, further entrenching gendered stereotypes. These issues persist despite the growing recognition that gender is not a binary construct. Accordingly, we should recognize that many AI systems were not designed to reflect this spectrum and embrace this inclusivity.

While we have little to no control over how AI systems are trained, we can take steps to identify and address bias in the outputs. By critically examining AI-generated results for patterns of bias, such as stereotypes or underrepresentation, we can better understand the system's limitations. Crafting prompts that explicitly challenge biases or request inclusive perspectives can help mitigate some of the harmful effects.

PERSONALIZED LEARNING

While the ethical challenges of AI in education, bias, privacy concerns, and the digital divide demand serious attention, they also underscore the importance of approaching AI integration with care and intentionality. These challenges highlight the central question brought up earlier in the chapter: Who benefits and who gets left behind? Personalized learning offers a compelling answer. With tools like ChatGPT, Claude, and others, we can move beyond one-size-fits-all instruction, creating adaptive experiences that meet students where they are.

Personalized learning at its core is about adaptability, tailoring educational experiences to the unique needs, preferences, and pace of individual learners. It represents a shift from traditional, uniform teaching methods to a more dynamic approach that evolves in response to student progress and feedback. Generative AI enhances this adaptability by helping you analyze student interactions and dynamically adjust its responses to better meet their evolving needs. Whether you're crafting study materials aligned to a student's specific knowledge gap or providing more timely feedback that resonates with their learning style, these tools make individualized teaching possible and practical.

Leveraging Large Language Models in Personalized Learning

Large language models (LLMs) like ChatGPT have introduced a paradigm shift in how personalized learning can be implemented by instructors. These systems allow educators to craft tailored experiences that directly address individual student needs.

LLMs stand out particularly in their ability to understand context, generate tailored responses, facilitate adaptive feedback, and engage in conversational learning. Let's look at how instructors can engage with these tools to accelerate the development of personalized learning materials.

Understand Context

These models analyze the input provided and generate responses that consider the broader context. Meaning, a question about "pH levels" in a biology assignment will yield a different response than the same question framed within a chemistry discussion. The key is to make sure you provide enough information in your prompt for the tool to differentiate them. In this case, it would be very helpful to include an assignment description when you begin your conversation with the chatbot.

Example Prompt: I'm working on a biology assignment where students need to analyze how pH levels affect enzyme activity. Can you help me create a discussion question that encourages critical thinking and connects to real-world applications?

Generate Tailored Responses

You can enable responses that are dynamically aligned with specific learning objectives and individual student queries. A student struggling with understanding how to solve quadratic equations might receive a step-by-step breakdown of the process, including worked examples, while an advanced student would be challenged with real-world application problems that require creative problem solving.

Facilitate Adaptive Feedback

These tools can provide real-time feedback that is specific and constructive, such as highlighting errors in a student's argument and suggesting ways to strengthen it. An English instructor could use ChatGPT to evaluate a student's essay on literary analysis. The tool might point out issues like where the thesis statement lacks clarity or where evidence isn't well-connected to the argument. The instructor could then guide it to suggest strategies to rephrase content or include additional examples to strengthen the analysis.

Engage in Conversational Learning

LLMs can also simulate one-on-one tutoring by engaging in dialogue that evolves based on student input. For example, a student preparing for an English literature exam might prompt an LLM with "Explain how symbolism is used in *The Great Gatsby* with examples." The LLM will respond with a tailored explanation, highlighting key symbols like the green light and its significance in the novel's themes. Instructors can encourage students to use LLMs this way by integrating such prompts into learning activities, teaching them to refine their queries to extract deeper insights or add clarity for elements of complicated topics.

Integration Into Personalized Learning

Unlike pre-built platforms that offer limited customization, LLMs provide faculty with the flexibility to design highly tailored educational experiences, and instructors should focus on mastering the practical steps of interacting with AI tools to develop learning experiences.

- **Craft Specific Prompts:** Detailed and precise prompts yield the most useful outputs. Instead of asking "Explain photosynthesis," try "Explain photosynthesis to a 10th-grade biology class, including an analogy and key terms."

- **Review Outputs Critically:** While LLMs are powerful, their responses aren't always accurate and can subtly hallucinate. Educators should verify and adjust the content as needed.
- **Engage Students Actively:** Encourage students to use LLMs as learning partners, teaching them to ask follow-up questions and refine their inquiries for better insights if the output doesn't meet their expectations.

Let's explore how those unique capabilities can be applied in practical and impactful ways within the classroom. By focusing on adaptable strategies, educators can harness these tools to design personalized and meaningful learning experiences for their students. All the examples below can be applied to LLMs like ChatGPT, Claude, Copilot, and Gemini.

- **Custom Study Guides:** Create bespoke study materials based on class notes or lecture transcripts that you upload to ChatGPT.

  Prompt: I'm teaching an undergraduate American history course. Create a study guide for the Civil Rights Movement, including key events, figures, and their impacts. [Include course materials related to the subject.]

  The generated content can then be refined further to align with course objectives. If you find content is missing in the output, adjust your prompt to explicitly include those elements.

- **Dynamic Question Generation:** Generate practice questions tailored to individual learning goals.

  Prompt: Write three multiple-choice questions on Newton's laws of motion, varying in difficulty, and include detailed explanations for each answer.

  This gives you the opportunity to provide diverse practice opportunities without having to create everything from scratch.

- **Personalized Feedback:** When considering uploading student-created content to third-party systems, caution is warranted as companies may use this data for training future models. These files should always be anonymized. Understand that companies like Google or OpenAI will then use student work to train future models. Educators should consult with legal experts at their organization for additional policy guidance. If you decide to use AI for personal feedback, consider using this prompt when a student submits an essay:

  Prompt: Analyze this essay for coherence, argument strength, and grammar, and suggest improvements.

This approach complements the instructor's insights, saving time while maintaining quality. *It's best to avoid asking ChatGPT to generate feedback that appears to come from you personally.*

- **Language Support and Accessibility:** These models can help bridge language barriers by translating course materials or providing explanations in simpler language for students with different proficiency levels. For example, a monolingual English-speaking teacher could use an AI tool to help interpret and provide feedback on a student's assignment that includes both English and Spanish. The AI can assist in identifying the meaning and intent behind translanguaging, allowing the teacher to respond thoughtfully without needing to be fluent in both.

  Prompt: Explain the concept of entropy in simple terms for an undergraduate student.

- **Facilitating Collaborative Learning:** Group activities can be supported by generating prompts or discussion guides that cater to varying perspectives within a group.

  Prompt: Create a debate outline where one side defends the Industrial Revolution as a net positive for society, and the other argues its negative impacts, providing points for each side.
  Prompt: Draft a list of open-ended questions that could guide a group discussion on the ethical implications of AI in the workplace for an undergraduate business course.

Case: Adapting Algebra Exercises With a Large Language Model

Professor Ramirez teaches intermediate algebra to undergraduate students with varied backgrounds. Some barely passed high school math, while others are returning to college after years away. She wants to give students personalized practice without overwhelming or boring them.

Exploring the potential of large language models, she begins experimenting with ChatGPT. She quickly notices that vague prompts yield unhelpful responses, so she starts refining them with specific learning goals in mind.

For example:

- **Student A** struggles with factoring. The model offers step-by-step guidance, flags common errors, and includes self-check problems.
- **Student B** already has the basics down. ChatGPT provides advanced practice framed in real-world applications like budgeting and break-even analysis.
- **Student C** doesn't know how to ask effective questions. Professor Ramirez models a prompt: "Explain how to factor a quadratic in vertex form and give a practice problem involving a real-life scenario." The model replies with a clear explanation and a projectile motion word problem.

She also uses ChatGPT for biweekly reflection assignments. Students submit short summaries of confusing topics. If the summaries are unclear, the model responds with questions to help them clarify their thinking: "Is the issue with grouping terms or recognizing perfect squares?" Professor Ramirez uses these exchanges to help students identify and articulate problem areas.

Over time, students learn to write better prompts. When they clearly explain what they're stuck on, such as "I'm confused about the last step in completing the square," the AI responds more precisely. The result is more relevant practice and better feedback.

Key Takeaway: Clear prompts and context are vital for effective use of large language models like ChatGPT. By helping students develop strong questions, you can support more personalized practice, reflective learning, and targeted feedback.

AI-Driven Content Creation

Creating engaging course materials is essential for good teaching, but as you know, it's incredibly time-consuming. AI tools now offer you ways to craft custom content that speaks directly to student needs, thereby allowing you to focus on students, not documents.

These tools can generate interactive quizzes, flash cards, custom textbooks, and adaptive content that meets different learning styles. For example, Beautiful.ai is a free online app that helps you build professional-looking slide decks quickly by turning your input, such as text, bullet points, or outlines, into visually engaging presentations. You can use it to create an entire lecture presentation from your course materials in minutes, which frees up more time for class preparation.

When deciding which content to create with AI assistance, the TPACK framework offers valuable guidance. Your technological knowledge of AI capabilities combined with your pedagogical understanding and subject expertise helps you choose where AI adds the most value. For instance, AI might generate practice problems, but you'll need to verify accuracy and determine appropriate difficulty levels.

For specific student challenges, AI can provide targeted solutions. Think of a nursing professor using ChatGPT to create a pharmacology study guide. They would get started by simply entering a prompt like "Create a personalized study guide on pharmacology for undergraduate nursing students with simplified explanations of drug classifications, side effects, and practice questions."

The result is a comprehensive guide with clear classifications, examples, mechanisms of action, and side effects. All this output is easily modifiable through follow-up prompts, enabling struggling students to tackle more complex material.

Keeping Content Current

Keeping your course materials fresh and relevant can feel like an uphill battle, especially when student needs and academic standards are always changing.

Fortunately, these tools offer a practical solution, which enables educators to update resources dynamically and keep them aligned with current expectations.

As someone who reflects often on my own teaching outcomes, I know these tools excel at processing learner feedback to identify areas where improvements are needed. These tools can highlight patterns and provide actionable insights.

- **Identifying Common Challenges:** If students frequently miss the same quiz question, an instructor can use ChatGPT to review the question and its related material. By prompting with "Rewrite this quiz question to make the concept of photosynthesis clearer for students who are struggling," the instructor can quickly refine the question and address the root cause of confusion.
- **Adjusting Content in Real Time:** By analyzing student performance trends and consulting AI, educators can receive tailored recommendations. Ask "Suggest supplemental resources for students struggling to understand cellular respiration," and use the generated suggestions to create targeted materials, such as explainer videos or alternative practice exercises.
- **Monitoring Changes:** Using tools like Perplexity, a free AI-powered search engine that pulls information from current web sources, educators can monitor updates to curriculum requirements or accreditation standards. For example, a biology instructor can go to Perplexity and ask "What are the latest updates to AP Biology curriculum guidelines?" to check that their materials align with the most recent standards.
- **Proposing Relevant Updates:** Tools like ScholarAI, a browser extension that connects ChatGPT to peer-reviewed academic research, can suggest specific enhancements to course materials by analyzing current studies and trends. A psychology professor could prompt ScholarAI with "Provide recent case studies on cognitive behavioral therapy interventions for adolescent anxiety" and receive curated, up-to-date content to enrich their lectures and assignments.

Keeping educational content current is about creating a meaningful and impactful learning experience. By leveraging AI to manage time-consuming updates and analyses, educators can focus on engaging with their students and delivering relevant instruction that meets today's standards.

Balancing Automation With Human Oversight

As educators, we're always looking for tools to help us work smarter. AI has opened doors to automation that can save time and enhance learning, but we need to strike the right balance between technology and human expertise. The educator's role isn't about stepping back but stepping in with intention for our students.

While AI tools excel at generating discussion questions and study materials, you should still review, refine, and align the content with specific learning objectives to maintain accuracy and relevance. A well-crafted prompt is just the beginning. Instructor oversight helps align the content with educational goals and supports meaningful engagement.

Consider how a history instructor might use Claude, an AI chatbot developed by Anthropic that's designed to be conversational and thoughtful in its responses, to generate discussion questions about the Industrial Revolution. By refining the initial prompt to include specific pedagogical goals like "emphasizing critical thinking and primary source analysis," the instructor can transform basic questions into more sophisticated prompts that encourage deeper historical inquiry and methodological awareness. Give it a try and see how much richer your class discussions can become.

Two key strategies help maintain this balance:

1. *Human in the Loop*: Positioning the educator as an active participant in the AI workflow, evaluating and modifying output rather than allowing the AI to operate autonomously.
2. *Human-Augmented Intelligence*: Using AI to amplify human skills, provide insights, and streamline complex tasks, allowing educators to focus on areas requiring judgment and higher-order thinking.

In practice, these strategies work together in adaptive learning environments. Think about how you can use AI to identify struggling students. It can also suggest resources, augmenting your ability to target teaching efforts effectively. You would then need to review this analysis to verify its accuracy against known course challenges and make the necessary adjustments. Doing this helps keep the technology aligned with your pedagogical goals rather than letting it drive them.

AI will continue to quickly evolve, and so will the opportunities to use it. The way we approach this evolution matters. By embedding ethical considerations into every aspect of AI use, from content creation to personalized learning, we can create a future where technology enhances the human elements of teaching and learning.

Let's commit to being thoughtful stewards of this technology. Let's use it to amplify our efforts, not replace them. And let's remember the goal of education isn't just to teach content, it's to empower students, build connections, and foster understanding in ways that only humans can.

DISCUSSION AND ACTIVITY

Discussion

AI technology has opened exciting possibilities in education, requiring critical examination of how these tools impact students and learning environments. Use these discussion points for personal reflection or classroom conversations about the ethical challenges of AI-driven personalization.

Addressing Bias in AI Outputs

AI systems reflect biases present in their training data, often favoring Western perspectives, standard English dialects, and dominant cultural frameworks.

Reflection prompt: Think of a time when you encountered content that didn't reflect your cultural perspective or background. How did this affect your learning experience? What about it made you feel included or excluded?

Questions to Explore:

1. Educator obligations regarding AI bias:
   » What is an instructor's duty to review AI outputs?
   » How can we balance efficiency with equity?
   » What strategies help identify subtle forms of bias?
2. Preparing students as critical AI consumers:
   » How can we teach bias recognition skills and cultural awareness?
   » What approaches encourage students to question AI outputs and express diverse perspectives?
3. Practical strategies for mitigating AI bias:
   » How can we create diverse prompt examples that incorporate multiple cultural perspectives?
   » What methods support various English dialects and writing styles?

Balancing Privacy and AI Integration

When AI tools are used, student data may be collected and utilized in ways not fully understood. Many platforms incorporate user interactions to train future models, often without explicit consent, raising ethical concerns around consent and transparency.

Reflection Prompts:

- What personal or professional information would you be uncomfortable sharing with an AI system?
- How do you decide which digital tools to trust with your data?

Questions to Explore:

1. Appropriate AI tool requirements:
   » Under what circumstances should instructors require AI tool usage, given privacy concerns?
   » How do we evaluate educational value against privacy risks?
   » What alternative approaches might achieve similar learning outcomes?

2. Institutional frameworks for responsible AI use:
   » What guidelines, vetting processes, and data protection standards are needed?
   » What training should educators receive for responsible AI integration?
3. Long-term implications:
   » How might current AI usage decisions affect student trust, future educational tools, and relationships between institutions and tech companies?

Activity

One effective way to use AI in teaching is to improve assignment descriptions for inclusivity. This approach can be particularly valuable for supporting nontraditional students and promoting equitable learning experiences. Even without expertise in inclusive design, AI can help identify improvements to make your materials more accessible to all students.

Example Process

Original Assignment (Before):
Research Paper: Technology's Impact on Society

Write a 2,000-word research paper analyzing how a specific technology has impacted society. Include at least five scholarly sources from academic journals. Your paper should follow APA format and include an introduction, literature review, analysis, and conclusion.

The AI-Assisted Improvement Process:

1. Input a prompt like "I teach a population of nontraditional college students. I'm interested in making one of my assignments more inclusive. The assignment is below; please look at it and offer suggestions to improve it. [Paste in assignment description.]"
2. The AI will suggest improvements focused on:
   » Transparent purpose and task breakdown
   » Support and scaffolding
   » Expanding source requirements
   » Offering a transparent grading rubric

Key Improvements in the Revised Assignment:

- Added a clear purpose statement explaining the assignment's goals and benefits
- Detailed task breakdown with explicit section descriptions

- Expanded instructions with concrete examples and scaffolded steps
- Support resources identified for potentially challenging aspects
- Transparent grading criteria outlining specific assessment factors
- Accessible language throughout with a supportive, encouraging tone

Your Task

- Identify an assignment from your course that could benefit from greater inclusivity.
- Use AI to analyze your assignment and suggest improvements.
- Adapt the suggestions to create a more inclusive version that addresses:
    a. Clarity of purpose and expectations.
    b. Support for learner needs.
    c. Accessibility of language and requirements.
    d. Transparency in evaluation criteria.

Once you've selected an assignment, draft a revised version using the ideas shown in the example above. If you're unsure where to start or would like fresh ideas, use AI to analyze your original assignment and suggest improvements.

CHAPTER 5

Crafting AI-Driven Assessments

Creating Fair and Effective Evaluations With AI

FOUNDATIONS OF ASSESSMENT DESIGN

Introduction

In summer 2023, as universities scrambled to address the changes AI would bring, the dean of our College of Health Sciences called me. She invited me to her retreat to brief her executive committee on AI breakthroughs and preparation strategies. The dean and I work well together, and she approaches technology with forward-thinking pragmatism.

When I present, I focus on two key elements: answering "So what?" by connecting directly to my audience's concerns and providing tangible solutions to the problems I address.

The "so what" seemed obvious. Faculty and leadership across the university asked one burning question: How would AI impact student assessment? How could we verify student learning if AI could answer everything for them? The solution proved far more challenging. How could we modify assessments to respond to AI's capabilities?

I gathered our instructional design team to develop strategies to help faculty create effective assessments in the AI era. We quickly realized one important truth: that we couldn't "AI-proof" anything. Instead, we needed to create "AI-informed" assessments.

After intensive work, we developed a process to reshape assignments for the AI revolution. At the retreat, I showed the executive team how thoughtfully applied AI could improve teaching and how to update assessment practices to accurately measure student learning. Now I'll share these AI-informed assessment practices with you.

Moving Beyond Traditional Assessment: The AI Transformation

For decades, assessment followed a predictable formula: fixed-structure exams, standardized tests, and uniform rubrics designed for efficiency. These traditional models, while practical for large-scale administration, fail to capture the nuances of student learning and present several critical limitations:

- Standardized tests assume all students demonstrate knowledge identically. They neglect diverse learning styles and alternative ways to show mastery. A student who struggles with timed multiple-choice tests might excel in problem solving or portfolio-based evaluation, yet traditional assessments rarely accommodate this flexibility.
- These tests reward fact recall rather than critical thinking, encouraging students to focus on test-taking strategies instead of developing conceptual understanding. Real-world success demands the application of knowledge, not just the recitation of isolated facts.
- Summative assessments like final exams and papers serve as endpoints, assigning grades without meaningful guidance on improvement. Students miss chances to refine their understanding before moving forward.

AI now invites us to reimagine our approach to assessment. The traditional assessment model may no longer fully align with education's adaptive, iterative nature in today's world. With the emergence of generative AI, educators have an opportunity to develop assessments that:

- Shift from summative to formative evaluation
    - » Instead of treating assessments solely as final judgments, treat them as ongoing learning experiences that provide timely feedback and allow for refinement before final submission.
- Emphasize higher-order thinking
    - » Education today benefits when students analyze, synthesize, and apply information in complex ways. Open-ended problem solving, scenario-based challenges, and interactive simulations can serve as valuable tools that measure skills beyond what AI might easily replicate.

When ChatGPT first emerged, many instructors initially sought ways to "AI-proof" their assessments. Experience has shown that this approach may not be the most effective strategy for long-term educational goals. A more forward-thinking strategy acknowledges students' access to AI and integrates it responsibly into the assessment process. This shift encourages critical engagement with AI rather than blind reliance or attempted avoidance.

The new assessment paradigm emphasizes:

- Process over product
    - » Assessments can benefit from including drafts, revisions, and reasoning behind student work, rather than focusing exclusively on polished final versions.
- Reflective practice
    - » Incorporating opportunities for students to document AI use, evaluate AI-generated responses, and critique their accuracy may deepen their engagement with the material.

- Real-world application
    - » Case studies, debates, and complex problem-solving tasks tend to foster independent thought and practical application that extends beyond static evaluations.

AI challenges us to design assessments that move beyond simple recall, incorporating real-time feedback and embracing diverse ways for students to demonstrate mastery. The future of assessment lies not in resisting AI's advance but in harnessing its potential to create more authentic, dynamic, and effective evaluation methods.

This transition from traditional to AI-informed assessment models reflects key principles of the TPACK framework. As you redesign assessments, consider how AI tools complement your teaching methods and subject matter goals rather than simply adding technology because it's the hot thing to do. This TPACK-guided approach helps create assessments that measure meaningful learning while acknowledging the realities of an AI-enabled educational landscape.

Applying the Transparency in Learning and Teaching (TILT) Framework

If you've ever given an assignment and received wildly off-base submissions, you know how much confusion unclear expectations can create. Students aren't mind readers, and sometimes what seems obvious to an instructor is anything but to the learner. That's where the TILT framework, a straightforward, research-backed approach to making learning expectations crystal clear, comes in.

Developed by Dr. Mary-Ann Winkelmes (Winkelmes, 2013), TILT was designed to help students, particularly those from underrepresented and first-generation backgrounds, navigate academic expectations more effectively. At its core, TILT is about breaking down assignments and assessments into three essential components: Purpose, Task, and Criteria for Success. By making each of these elements explicit, educators reduce ambiguity and improve student engagement (TILT Higher Ed., n.d.).

Purpose

The first component, *Purpose*, is all about helping students understand why they're doing a particular assignment. Too often, students approach tasks as meaningless hoops to jump through. They are simply checking boxes. But when educators articulate the connection between an assignment and learning objectives, real-world applications, or skill development, students build connections and engage more meaningfully. Instead of simply telling them to write a research paper, an instructor using TILT would explain that the assignment develops critical thinking, argumentation skills, and the ability to synthesize information, skills that are valuable in professional and academic settings alike.

Task

The second element, *Task*, provides students with a clear roadmap for completing the assignment. This goes beyond a vague directive and instead offers step-by-step instructions that eliminate confusion. A well-structured task description helps students to understand exactly what is expected, what materials they need, and how they should approach the work. This clarity is especially important when AI is involved. Students often benefit from clear guidance regarding how AI tools might be appropriately used, whether for brainstorming, drafting, or analyzing data. Without clear task instructions, students may misuse AI or fail to develop the critical skills the assignment is meant to assess.

Criteria for Success

Finally, *Criteria for Success* helps students understand what high-quality work looks like before they begin. Rather than guessing what an instructor values, students are given explicit grading rubrics, sample responses, or exemplars that model successful outcomes. This level of transparency helps level the playing field, particularly for students who may not have been exposed to the unspoken rules of academic success. When incorporating AI-informed assessments, Criteria for Success would include examples of strong analytical reasoning, originality in thought, and appropriate AI integration that can help students better navigate ethical and academic integrity expectations.

Using the TILT framework in AI-informed assessments helps students turn in better work and transform their approach to learning. With clear expectations, they can focus on the substance of their ideas rather than second-guessing instructions. They will know how to use AI appropriately, where to apply their own critical thinking, and how to produce work that meets high academic standards.

Applying TILT to AI-Informed Assessments

Incorporating AI into assessments transforms the learning experience but requires explicit guidelines to avoid confusion. The TILT framework provides the perfect structure for these AI-enhanced assignments.

When AI enters the assessment picture, providing clarity about purpose becomes one of our most important tasks. Students should understand not only why an assessment matters for their grade but how it connects to real-world applications and course objectives. Strive to explicitly address AI's role: Is it permitted? For which parts? Should students use it for brainstorming, drafting, or refinement? If you restrict AI, it's critical to explain your rationale. Perhaps the assignment aims to build individual problem-solving skills that AI would undermine. This transparency prevents misuse and promotes intentional engagement.

Consider outlining which parts students might complete manually versus where they may employ AI tools. Clear parameters for AI use could be helpful:

You might consider whether students should cite AI-generated content. Should they compare AI outputs with their own analysis? These specifications help students view AI more as a learning tool.

Your rubrics should also define success both in traditional terms like originality, coherence, and depth of thought, and in relation to AI use. Specify how students should demonstrate critical engagement. Should they reflect on AI-generated content? Show evidence of revisions? Explain how AI influenced their work? Provide examples that match these criteria to set clear benchmarks.

The TILT framework transforms AI-informed assessments by making AI expectations explicit and applying consistent criteria for all students, regardless of their familiarity with AI. Through providing clarity about purpose, task, and evaluation criteria, TILT creates a transparent environment where students understand how to appropriately integrate AI into their academic work.

Case: Revising a Writing Assignment With TILT and AI

Professor Chen teaches Introduction to Political Theory, a writing-intensive course for 1st-year students. For years, she assigned a classic midterm prompt: "Write a five-page essay analyzing how Hobbes and Locke differ in their views of human nature." Students often struggled with structure and clarity, and Professor Chen spent hours giving feedback on basic writing mechanics rather than engaging ideas.

Curious about generative AI, she updated the assignment for this semester but didn't change her instructions. Some students used ChatGPT for outlining, grammar checks, and even initial drafts. Others avoided it entirely, unsure whether it was allowed. The results were uneven. Some essays were polished but generic. Others showed strong ideas but were hard to follow. Several students said they were confused about how and whether they were supposed to use AI at all.

For the final paper, Professor Chen decided to apply the TILT framework to clarify expectations and help students connect why this topic is important to understand. Here's how she revised the assignment:

- **Purpose:** She began the prompt with a brief explanation: "This assignment builds your ability to compare political theories, make evidence-based arguments, and express complex ideas clearly. These skills apply to law, public service, and many research fields."
- **Task:** She explicitly outlined AI expectations: "You may use AI tools to help generate an outline, check grammar, or suggest phrasing. However, all interpretation, analysis, and comparisons must be your own. Include a brief AI Use Statement with your paper explaining how you used any AI tools and how you reviewed or revised their input."
- **Criteria for Success:** She revised the rubric to include both traditional elements (clarity, accuracy, strength of argument) and new ones: evidence of

revision, depth of analysis, and appropriate use of AI. She also provided two annotated samples showing how AI-generated drafts were improved through critical thinking.

Key Lesson: TILT spells out what students must do themselves and where AI can help, making sure AI never overshadows their own reasoning. By drawing clear lines around student-led thinking versus AI assistance, you guide them to focus on their arguments while using AI for support. This clarity prevents shortcuts and keeps genuine inquiry at the heart of the assignment.

Leveraging AI to Make Assessments Aligned With Learning Objectives

AI itself can be a powerful tool in designing assessments that align directly with course learning outcomes. AI-generated questions, prompts, and rubrics can be fine-tuned to match frameworks like Bloom's Taxonomy, a framework for categorizing levels of thinking, from remembering to creating (Anderson et al., 2001). This helps assessments measure not just recall but also application, analysis, and evaluation skills. You can also use an AI tool to analyze existing assessments to identify gaps or areas where evaluation criteria may not fully align with learning objectives.

Beyond design, AI increases transparency in assessment delivery. AI tools can generate structured instructions that help you to clarify purpose, expectations, and evaluation criteria. Additionally, rubrics created with AI assistance can help refine grading standards so that students know exactly how their work will be evaluated from the start. We'll look more closely at these elements later in the chapter.

PROMOTING FAIRNESS IN AI-INFORMED ASSESSMENTS

As AI continues to shape education, its role in assessments brings both opportunities and challenges. Assessments built or integrated with AI raise important concerns about fairness. Promoting fairness means implementing these systems in ways that don't disadvantage or favor certain students based on factors unrelated to their actual performance. Biases, lack of contextual understanding, and opaque decision-making processes can all contribute to unfair outcomes.

Faculty Concerns and Roles

AI-assisted assessments promise efficiency, personalization, and valuable insights into student learning. However, faculty rightly have concerns about protecting academic integrity, maintaining rigor, and using AI responsibly. Thoughtful implementation is crucial to prevent AI from enabling academic dishonesty, diluting learning experiences, or creating an overreliance on automation.

Ensure Integrity

There's a valid concern that in an AI-rich environment, students may be more tempted to submit AI-generated responses as their own. While this risk isn't caused by instructors using AI to design assessments, it does highlight the importance of creating assignments that encourage original thinking and make misuse easier to detect. However, rather than worrying about having to detect plagiarism retroactively, you can design assessments that encourage original thought and transparency in AI use.

Instead of banning AI outright, consider requiring students to document how they used AI in their work. Think about how a history professor might ask students to submit a reflective piece alongside their essay. Within that reflection they would have the opportunity to explain how they used AI tools for assistance. Below are the types of questions students should consider:

- What specific aspects of your writing did AI help with?
- How did you evaluate the AI's suggestions for accuracy and relevance?
- What changes did you make after receiving AI-generated feedback?

Maintaining Rigor

A common worry is that AI-enhanced assessments will simplify learning, making assignments less intellectually demanding. We need to design assessments that require students to think beyond what AI can produce. The tools should not open avenues to replace critical thinking.

Alongside the artifact of learning students develop, they should be ready to:

- Critically evaluate AI-recommended sources for credibility and bias.
- Compare AI summaries to original content to identify missing nuances.
- Use AI to generate counterarguments and then respond to them with original analysis.

Understanding AI's Assessment Limitations

Despite AI's analytical capabilities, it falls short in crucial assessment areas where human judgment remains irreplaceable. AI-generated numerical grades lack reliability because these models don't truly "understand" student work but rather simply predict scores based on patterns. These educated guesses lead to inconsistent evaluation and obscure the rationale behind grades.

AI particularly struggles with complex, creative work that defies conventional patterns. Consider a student who blends philosophy, sociology, and literature in a novel argument about urban development. An AI system might penalize this interdisciplinary approach because it doesn't match the predefined structures in its training data.

Another critical limitation appears in tracking student growth. AI systems typically evaluate each of your submissions in isolation, failing to recognize a student's development over time. When a student who struggled with thesis development earlier in the semester finally masters this skill, AI won't recognize and reward this breakthrough by comparing this student's newer writing to previous work.

Human instructors excel precisely where AI falters by evaluating unconventional approaches, recognizing cross-disciplinary insights, appreciating creative expression, and acknowledging personal growth. These elements form the heart of meaningful assessment and cannot be automated without sacrificing the very qualities we seek to develop in our students.

Maintain Instructor Presence

When AI dominates the assessment process, critical aspects of learning suffer. Its feedback often lacks the personalized touch that addresses individual student growth. It struggles to interpret creative or unconventional approaches, potentially misclassifying innovative work as incorrect. Perhaps most concerning, overreliance on AI weakens the faculty–student connection that drives trust and motivation.

When aiming to preserve meaningful human presence while leveraging the advantages AI has to offer, consider exploring these high-impact strategies:

1. **Strategic Personalized Follow-Up:** Adding context-specific comments throughout AI-generated feedback can help create connections to individual students. Rather than duplicating what the AI provides, focus on insights that reflect your expertise and knowledge of the student's progress. A brief note about how a student's current work builds on their previous submissions demonstrates attentiveness that AI cannot replicate.
2. **Design Interactive Assessment Touchpoints:** Considering assignments that include direct faculty–student interaction can help maintain meaningful educational connections. Incorporate oral presentations, staged project milestones, or structured discussions that place you at the center of the learning process. These elements promote direct interaction between you and students, moving beyond automated systems.
3. **Build Reflective Dialogue Opportunities:** Small-group debrief sessions where students can discuss their experiences with AI-informed assessments might offer valuable insights. These conversations transform assessment from a one-way judgment into a collaborative learning opportunity where you guide students in understanding not just what they produced but how they can improve their process.

AI works best when it handles routine tasks, freeing you to focus on the human elements of teaching. The goal isn't to compete with AI but to direct it strategically.

Data Privacy in AI-Driven Assessments

As discussed in more detail in Chapter 4, data privacy remains one of the most pressing concerns when integrating AI into educational settings. When it comes to AI-powered assessment tools, the trade-off often comes in the form of data ingestion. These systems collect, analyze, and store student information in ways that are sometimes unclear or undisclosed. Faculty should try to stay informed about how these tools handle student work, metadata, and personal information to stay compliant with legal standards and uphold their ethical obligations to students.

Understanding the Risks

A significant problem we face with these platforms is the lack of transparency about how they handle data. Some tools may store student responses indefinitely while using them to train future models without consent. Others may not clearly disclose their methodologies or weighting algorithms, which leaves us in the dark about how decisions are made. This lack of transparency raises serious ethical concerns. Students deserve to know where their data is going and if their work is being used to develop a product for yet another tech firm.

In the United States, the Family Educational Rights and Privacy Act (FERPA) gives parents and eligible students the right to access and control their educational records. This means that when these systems are used in the classroom, they must incorporate safeguards that limit data access and sharing to situations with explicit consent or legally defined exceptions. Similarly, the General Data Protection Regulation (GDPR) in the European Union mandates that any collection, processing, or storage of personal data—including data processed by artificial intelligence—must adhere to strict principles like data minimization and purpose limitation. Under GDPR, institutions must clearly communicate how student data is used, provide easy avenues for consent, and allow individuals to exercise their rights to access, correct, or delete their data.

Best Practices for Privacy and Security

AI assessment tools require student data, creating privacy and security concerns that demand your attention. To protect student information while leveraging its benefits, focus on these essential practices:

- **Choose Vetted Tools With Clear Policies:** It's good practice to select AI platforms that have received institutional approval and offer transparent privacy policies for additional security. Before integrating tools into your course, you might consider reviewing how each handles, stores, and processes student data.
- **Minimize Data Exposure:** It's generally advisable to avoid uploading personally identifiable student information to AI tools without explicit

permission. Using anonymized data when possible and collecting only what's essential for your educational objectives helps to protect student privacy.

- **Offer Student Choice:** Considering alternatives for students who may feel uncomfortable with AI-driven assessments could be beneficial. Opt-out options for these assignments might demonstrate respect for student autonomy regarding how their data is used.
- **Maintain Transparency:** Providing clear explanations to students about data collection practices, including what data is collected, the purpose behind collection, and protection measures, can help build trust.
- **Document Your Practices:** Keeping records of student data collection, usage patterns, and obtained consent can support legal compliance efforts.

Where Bias Creeps Into Assessment

AI has the power to promise efficiency when you're developing assessments, but AI systems aren't immune to bias. In fact, they often reinforce the same biases that traditional assessments have struggled with, just faster and at scale.

Bias in Writing and Essay Evaluation

These tools reward formulaic writing. They favor structured, predictable essays with clear thesis statements, topic sentences, and linear arguments. That's great for students trained to write in a standard academic format, but what about those who take a more creative approach? Students who use storytelling techniques, indirect argumentation, or rhetorical structures rooted in their cultural backgrounds may find their work penalized, not because of poor reasoning but because AI doesn't recognize these structures as valid. Let's take a look:

Prompt: Please analyze these student essays about social media's impact on society. Evaluate their argument structure, evidence use, and overall effectiveness. Provide specific feedback for improvement.
Essay 1: Social media has three major impacts on modern society. First, it has changed how we communicate. Studies show that 85% of teens prefer texting to talking. Second, it has transformed business marketing. Companies now spend billions on digital advertising. Finally, it has altered political discourse through the spread of misinformation. These three factors demonstrate social media's profound influence on our world.
AI Feedback for Essay 1: Strong essay with excellent organization. The thesis clearly states three impacts, and each paragraph systematically develops one point. Good use of statistical evidence about teen communication preferences. Consider adding more specific examples for the marketing and political points. The conclusion effectively ties back to the thesis. To strengthen further, incorporate counterarguments and deeper analysis of each impact.

Essay 2: My grandmother used to tell stories on our front porch. Now she shares memes on Facebook. Her journey from oral storytelling to digital sharing mirrors our society's transformation. When I watch her scroll through her feed, posting photos and commenting on friends' updates, I see how social media hasn't just changed communication, it has reimagined it. The same platforms that let her stay connected with family have also become battlegrounds where marketers compete for attention and political truths blur into fiction.
AI Feedback for Essay 2: The essay lacks clear structure and needs a more explicit thesis statement. While the personal anecdote about your grandmother is interesting, it takes up too much space that could be used for direct analysis. The connection between storytelling and social media is unclear. Consider reorganizing to state your main points up front and use specific evidence rather than personal examples. The essay would benefit from a more academic approach with clear topic sentences and supporting evidence.

The AI praises the first essay's predictable structure while missing its superficial analysis. It dismisses the second essay's narrative approach, failing to recognize how the grandmother example effectively illustrates communication evolution. This bias discourages diverse writing styles, even when they convey complex ideas that align with assignment goals. If you're using ChatGPT or other generative AI tools to help you analyze essays, don't assume the feedback is fair.

Bias in Multiple-Choice Questioning

This same problem appears in AI-generated test questions, which often contain embedded assumptions about a student's background. Consider this nursing exam question:

Question: When you are providing discharge teaching to a patient who experienced a mild heart attack, which lifestyle modification should be emphasized first?

A. Joining a gym for regular exercise
B. Preparing heart-healthy meals at home
C. Reducing work-related stress
D. Following medication schedule

This seemingly straightforward question contains multiple biases:

- Options A and B assume financial means and time to join gyms or cook at home.
- Option B assumes kitchen access and control over meal preparation.
- Option C assumes traditional employment where stress control is possible.

While all modifications benefit heart health, the question advantages students who share middle-class assumptions about patient resources. Option D might seem the most universally applicable, but even it can pose challenges for patients who struggle to afford medications. The other options are even more likely to cause students to second-guess themselves based on their own socio-economic experiences.

Try not to assume AI feedback or questions are inherently fair. Instead:

- Compare AI feedback with human responses across diverse student submissions.
- Look for patterns where multilingual students or unconventional approaches receive lower scores.
- Review AI-generated questions for assumptions about cultural background, economic status, or linguistic norms.
- Aim to create examples that are accessible across diverse cultural contexts.
- Remember that AI should support your assessment expertise.

A fair assessment challenges all students equally, not just those who match default assumptions or write in ways AI readily recognizes.

Auditing AI-Generated Assessments for Fairness

AI-created assessments require careful oversight to keep them fair and free from bias. Taking an active role in auditing these systems and their responses helps verify that AI-generated content aligns with course objectives and remains fair to students of diverse linguistic backgrounds, cultures, and learning styles. These test questions should be checked for biases that may disadvantage certain student groups. AI has the capacity to generate content in such a way that it leads to an overrepresentation of in-group perspectives while excluding others.

When using any AI tool to help create assessments, manually reviewing the output helps verify that questions are clear, inclusive, and reflect a range of global perspectives. AI will often default to familiar narratives unless prompted otherwise. It's equally valuable to confirm that the questions generated align with the topics you've covered in your course. Let's walk through an example:

Prompt: Generate five history exam questions on industrialization.
AI Output: What were the key economic impacts of industrialization in Britain? How did industrialization change labor conditions in the United States?

These questions aren't wrong, but they center industrialization as a primarily Western experience.

Revised Prompt: Generate five history exam questions on how industrialization shaped different regions of the world, with at least one question for each of the following regions: Asia, Africa, and Latin America.

Improved AI Output: What role did industrialization play in Japan's rise as a global power in the late 19th century? How did industrialization affect labor migration and urbanization in Brazil?

These revisions guide the AI toward a more balanced and inclusive assessment while keeping you in control of the scope. Double-checking that the content reflects what students have encountered in class helps create questions that feel more relevant and fair.

BEST PRACTICES FOR AI-INFORMED ASSESSMENTS

Why AI-Proofing Doesn't Work

Attempts to "AI-proof" assessments may look a lot like an unwinnable arms race. Students already access these tools routinely, just as they use Google or Microsoft Word. Rather than resist this reality, consider how to adapt to it. Modern workplaces already integrate AI across industries from health care to journalism. When we ban AI, we fail to prepare students for professional environments where AI literacy now counts as an essential skill.

Students sometimes respond to restrictions by finding workarounds instead of engaging with the material. They seek the path of least resistance to "check the box" for course requirements.

A more effective approach embraces AI as a learning partner. By shifting focus from product to process, we can create assessments that reveal students' thinking, not just their output. This approach:

- **Fosters discerning technology use:** Students learn when and how to apply AI tools appropriately and develop judgment about generated suggestions rather than accepting them blindly.
- **Develops higher-order thinking:** While AI excels at summarizing information, it struggles with creative insights and contextual analysis. Well-designed assignments challenge students to move beyond what AI generates, requiring them to synthesize perspectives and apply knowledge to complex scenarios.
- **Promotes transparency and accountability:** Instead of restrictive policies, require students to document their AI interactions. This builds an honest culture where students submit usage logs or annotated drafts that explain how AI shaped their work.

This model transforms assessment from a test of what students can memorize to an evaluation of how they think, solve problems, and exercise judgment. By addressing AI's presence head-on, we prepare students for a world where success depends on using technology wisely rather than shunning or avoiding it.

Designing AI-Informed Assessments: Practical Strategies

Assessments can be structured into multiple checkpoints such as brainstorming sessions, drafts, and reflective reviews, which helps students engage with material iteratively rather than rely on shortcuts. Encouraging students to critically evaluate AI outputs by analyzing strengths, weaknesses, and omissions in responses might lead to deeper engagement with the material.

Assignments that mirror real-world industry challenges tend to require depth and context that AI responses often lack, which can foster more authentic student engagement. This strategy requires students to refine and interpret information through real-world problem solving, which makes assessments resistant to superficial AI content. They become more meaningful when students are invited to connect learning to their own experiences and perspectives, making AI-generated work less applicable. AI cannot replicate these unique insights. I often joke that a student might use ChatGPT to create a personal story, but they must then remember and stick to it all semester!

Collaborative learning through group projects can effectively foster interaction and critique, creating learning experiences that benefit from human exchange. AI generates generic content that lacks the adaptive thinking needed for effective discussions and teamwork.

Incorporating research requirements into assessment processes may strengthen students' information literacy while highlighting the limitations of AI tools. When students incorporate credible sources, analyze different viewpoints, and provide citations, they build a better understanding of the subject while developing information literacy, which has never been more important. This process helps you to highlight AI's limitations and reinforces for students the value of human judgment in academic work.

Strategies for AI-Informed Assessment Design

Assessments should reflect how students think, apply knowledge, and solve problems, not just how well they can memorize facts (Ajjawi et al., 2023). In an AI-driven world, it's more difficult, if not impossible, for traditional recall-based tests to measure meaningful learning because they emphasize surface-level knowledge rather than in-depth conceptual understanding. Instead, authentic assessments should push students to analyze, synthesize, and justify their reasoning. When students are asked to apply knowledge to real-world scenarios, explain their thinking, and refine their understanding over time, they develop better skills that go beyond what AI can replicate.

Emphasize Evaluation of Process Over Product

We like to think that students learn more from the journey than from the final submission. When assessments focus only on polished products, they overlook how students think, adapt, and refine their work. AI-informed assessments should emphasize the learning process by incorporating multiple submission checkpoints and opportunities for reflection. This structure mirrors how professionals work and teaches that learning occurs in stages.

One effective strategy is to require students to document their progress across several phases of an assignment. For a research project, this might include submitting an annotated bibliography, outline, first draft, and final paper. For lab reports or scientific writing, students could turn in raw data, methodology drafts, analysis, and then the final report. Each stage offers a chance for feedback and helps students to engage with the material consistently, rather than relying on AI to generate last-minute submissions.

In writing courses, consider asking for early-stage materials such as story concepts or character sketches before students submit full drafts. This kind of iterative drafting encourages better thinking, continuous improvement, and authentic skill development. With each revision, students apply feedback, refine their ideas, and build confidence in their own voice.

No matter what you're teaching, structuring assessments to emphasize process helps you gain a clearer picture of how students learn. It promotes integrity, highlights growth, and shifts the focus from just getting it done to understanding how it gets done.

Use Scaffolding to Reinforce Learning Steps

Break assessments into smaller, structured tasks to help students build toward complex learning objectives. The TILT framework offers an excellent structure for these tasks. Creating assignments to include manageable steps with clear expectations and deadlines can support student progress. Providing explicit criteria gives students the opportunity to evaluate and refine their work before submission.

For example, for a case study analysis, you could ask students to first submit a problem statement, then develop and justify a solution, and finally reflect on their approach and alternatives. This structure keeps students engaged throughout, promotes critical thinking, and allows continuous feedback.

Assessing Decision-Making and Justification

Understanding why students make specific choices matters as much as the choices themselves. AI-informed assessments should require students to explain their reasoning throughout their work to develop critical thinking skills.

- Show Work and Explore Alternatives
    - » In coding or math, inviting students to show their work, explore multiple solutions, and justify their final approach can encourage thorough problem solving rather than just finding answers.

- Reflect on Process
    - » When students reflect on their decision-making, they often begin to recognize thinking patterns and develop strategies for improvement.

For programming courses where AI can easily generate code:

- Require Explanations
    - » Students might benefit from submitting written or oral explanations of their design choices, algorithms, and problem-solving strategies alongside their code.
- Video Walkthroughs
    - » Brief video recordings where students explain their code line by line can make thought processes visible and demonstrate understanding.
- Debugging Exercises
    - » Code with intentional bugs or inefficiencies offers students opportunities to identify, explain, and fix problems, helping assess their ability to analyze and improve code rather than just generate it.

These strategies foster meaningful assessments while encouraging students to engage with programming beyond simply producing functional code.

Incorporate Reflective Components

Reflection-based prompts can encourage students to analyze their learning journey, articulate key takeaways, and evaluate challenges they've encountered. Structuring this reflection often helps them engage more deeply with the process.

Guided reflection forms offer a structured framework for students to assess their work. Questions such as "What strategies did you use to overcome challenges?" and "Describe a mistake you encountered and how you addressed it" can prompt meaningful self-assessment.

A comprehensive reflection form should include:

- Project summary and key functionalities
- Initial planning and strategies to overcome challenges
- Major challenges encountered and how mistakes were addressed
- Key learnings and comparison of expectations versus outcomes
- Areas for improvement and action plans
- Additional thoughts about the learning experience

Reflection journals extend this practice by encouraging students to document thoughts throughout the project. Logging reflections at different milestones helps track growth and refine insights into a final self-assessment. This makes reflection a habitual part of learning rather than a one-time exercise.

Reflection becomes more meaningful for students when it's incorporated into graded milestones, reinforcing its importance. Consider assigning a portion of the project grade to self-assessment so that students take it seriously and engage with their learning process.

Engage Students in Scenario-Based Assessments

Scenario-based assessments offer dynamic problem-solving experiences beyond simple knowledge recall. These assessments challenge students to navigate realistic situations where they analyze information, make decisions, and justify conclusions.

Nursing students can engage with simulated patient interactions to assess symptoms, recommend treatments, and justify decisions based on medical knowledge. Literature students might participate in role-play discussions as fictional characters, debating moral dilemmas from a first-person perspective. AI can facilitate these simulations, but students must apply critical thinking to refine and personalize their input and determine if the AI is providing relevant responses.

Sample Prompt for Nursing: Create a realistic scenario for nursing students that simulates a patient interaction with detailed information about symptoms, medical history, and current condition. The student must analyze this data, determine a treatment plan, and justify their decisions using medical knowledge. Include AI-generated patient responses to create an interactive experience that challenges students to think critically.

Sample Prompt for Literature: Develop a scenario in which students take on the role of a character from [insert novel title studied in class]. Present a moral dilemma the character might plausibly face, and ask students to respond in character, explaining their choices using textual evidence and the character's established values and motivations. Include AI-generated responses from other characters to support an immersive, discussion-based assessment.

Transform Multiple-Choice Questions into Case Studies

Educators can transform standard multiple-choice questions into detailed case studies that require analysis and justification. Instead of a multiple-choice question like "What causes climate change?" challenge students to analyze a scenario with conflicting policy proposals and recommend solutions.

For example, convert the following basic question into a case study:

Which causes climate change?

A. Human activities
B. Natural weather patterns

C. Both A and B
D. None of the above

Prompt: Create a scenario with conflicting climate policy proposals where one group emphasizes human factors and other natural factors. Include data points, stakeholder perspectives, and potential outcomes. Ask students to analyze evidence and justify actions addressing complex climate change causes.

This shift from recall-based tests to AI-informed assessments tends to create more meaningful learning experiences. These strategies contribute to measuring true understanding rather than simple memorization. Designing assessments that prepare students for a future where knowing how to think becomes more valuable than knowing what to think represents an important educational adaptation.

How AI Can Help Maintain Alignment

When instructors design assessments, they don't always realize that the final products might not align with the course content or learning objectives. Misaligned assessments can create unnecessary obstacles for students and weaken the effectiveness of a course. But with the help of AI tools, you can more easily identify and fix those gaps.

One of AI's biggest advantages is its ability to analyze course learning objectives and generate relevant assessment questions. Instead of manually creating every question, you can use AI to suggest options tailored to specific learning goals. Assessments can then focus on key concepts and minimize misalignment. AI can also help you map assignments to course content and flag potential gaps. By reviewing syllabi, lecture notes, and assigned readings, AI can highlight areas where assessments don't fully cover key concepts. Then you can adjust your strategies and create more comprehensive evaluations.

Let's look at a common issue: assessments that emphasize memorization over analysis. Imagine a biology course that emphasizes an understanding of ecosystems and applies ecological principles to environmental problems. The instructor frequently discusses real-world cases like invasive species or climate change and encourages students to develop innovative conservation strategies. Yet if the final exam is filled with questions like "What is an ecosystem?" or "Name three invasive species," it won't reflect the focus of the course. This instructor could run those questions through ChatGPT and ask "Do these align with a course focused on application and analysis?" The tool can suggest revisions that better match their goals.

A similar misalignment happens when questions don't reflect the material students were actually taught. Let's say you're teaching a literature course centered on two novels, but a few final exam questions are pulled from a test bank covering a third book that's barely mentioned in class. Students would be justifiably confused. To prevent this, the instructor could upload the syllabus and a few assessments into a generative AI tool of their choice and ask it to identify any gaps between objectives and test items.

Learning objectives themselves can cause problems if they're too vague. A goal like "Understand Renaissance art" is difficult to assess. But "Analyze how Renaissance artists used perspective to create depth in paintings" offers a clearer target. Once you've revised your learning objectives, ask an AI tool to evaluate whether your assessments match the updated goals. This gives you a tighter feedback loop for aligning instruction and evaluation.

The alignment process becomes more effective when viewed through the TPACK lens. AI tools can analyze course materials and suggest assessment adjustments, but your pedagogical expertise and content knowledge remain essential for judging whether these suggestions truly meet your learning objectives. This balance between the technology and your knowledge creates assessments that are both AI-informed and authentically aligned with what students need to learn.

Example Workflow for Using AI to Check Assessment Alignment

- Gather all existing course materials and assessments, making sure they're up to date and clearly tied to your learning goals.
- Provide the AI tool with these materials, along with context about the course objectives and student audience.
- Prompt the AI to analyze how well each assessment aligns with your stated objectives, asking for specific feedback or gaps.
- Review the AI's observations, refine or adjust assessments as needed, and confirm each rubric element clearly reflects its corresponding objective.

Sample Alignment Prompt: Here are the assessments I currently use in my Introduction to Environmental Science course, along with my course objectives. [Insert assessment(s) and objectives. These could be file attachments.] Identify whether each assessment aligns with the intended learning outcomes. Highlight any areas where alignment is weak or missing, and suggest specific changes to the assessments to improve clarity or relevance.

These tools won't replace your judgment, but they will surface inconsistencies, offer suggestions, and save you time. The goal is to make sure that every quiz, project, and paper reinforces the concepts you've prioritized. Alignment shouldn't be left to chance. By embedding AI into this review process, you can shift from just diagnosing misalignment to actively repairing it.

USING AI TO DEVELOP RUBRICS

AI-generated or AI-improved rubrics can help standardize grading criteria and improve assessment transparency. When designed thoughtfully, these rubrics give both educators and students a clear understanding of expectations, reducing ambiguity in grading and feedback. Leveraging AI in rubric development can also save educators time while helping maintain consistency in evaluation.

Creating Detailed Rubrics That Align With Course Learning Objectives

A well-crafted rubric should be an extension of the course's learning objectives. AI tools can assist in generating rubric language that explicitly connects assignment criteria with intended outcomes. If one of your learning objectives focuses on developing critical analysis skills, an AI-generated rubric can emphasize criteria such as depth of argument, evidence integration, and logical coherence.

Consider this workflow for creating a rubric using AI:

1. Define Learning Objectives
   » Input the course learning objectives into an AI tool, and ask it to generate a rubric that aligns with those goals.
2. Specify Performance Levels
   » Request that AI create detailed descriptors for each level of performance, for example, Excellent, Proficient, Developing, Needs Improvement.
3. Refine Output
   » Review and modify the AI-generated rubric to reflect disciplinary expectations and the specific nuances of the assignment.

Example Prompt for AI-Generated Rubrics

You can use AI more effectively by crafting structured prompts that guide rubric generation. The quality of AI-generated rubrics depends heavily on the specificity of your prompt and the context you provide. For optimal results, include:

1. Your complete assignment description.
2. Course level and subject area.
3. Specific learning objectives.
4. Desired complexity level.

Here's an example:

Prompt: I am teaching an undergraduate course on [subject]. Generate a rubric for a [type of assignment] that assesses students on [key learning objectives]. Include four levels of performance (Excellent, Proficient, Developing, Needs Improvement) and provide clear criteria for each level. Check that the rubric aligns with Bloom's Taxonomy, emphasizing [specific cognitive skills]. Below is the assignment; please use it for context [insert assignment description].

This approach:

1. Grounds the AI in your actual assignment context rather than generating generic criteria.
2. Allows for more precise alignment between assessment criteria and learning goals.
3. Captures the true complexity and the requirements of your assignment.
4. Helps maintain academic rigor while providing clear guidance to students.

Common Pitfalls and How to Avoid Them

There are some common issues that faculty run into when creating AI-informed assessments or integrating AI into their workflows more generally. Let's look at those issues and explore how to avoid them.

Lack of Pedagogical Intent

While AI tools can easily generate multiple-choice questions, essay prompts, and case studies, they do not inherently understand your course's objectives unless you explicitly make them clear in your prompt.

These questions may:

- Be too simplistic, testing only surface-level recall.
- Be overly complex, asking students to analyze concepts they have not yet learned.
- Lack direct relevance to the material covered in class.

Without review, these assessments can lead to frustration among students and misalignment with your intended learning goals. Instead of relying solely on AI-generated questions, use them as a starting point and refine them to accurately measure comprehension and critical thinking.

Loss of Instructor Presence in Feedback

Generic, automated feedback often lacks nuance, encouragement, and specificity, making it less effective for student improvement. While AI quickly analyzes text and suggests comments, it often:

- Provides vague and repetitive feedback.
- Makes superficial observations that fail to engage with the student's unique response.
- Lacks warmth and encouragement.

If students receive only AI-generated feedback, they may feel disconnected, frustrated that the instructor doesn't care, and unsure of how to apply the suggestions effectively. Draft initial feedback with AI, but always personalize and refine it before sending it to students.

The Gray Area Between Assistance and Authorship

Some students are now using Grammarly or ChatGPT to refine wording or suggest improvements, while others generate entire responses and lightly edit them. Where is the ethical boundary? Is AI-enhanced writing collaboration or misrepresentation?

If AI-generated content is undetectable, does this create an unfair advantage for students who use AI effectively versus those who don't? Without clear guidelines, disparities in AI use could lead to inconsistent expectations and unintended academic dishonesty. Clearly articulating what constitutes appropriate AI assistance versus academic dishonesty can help students make better ethical choices. For instance, using AI to check grammar or clarify awkward phrasing may be appropriate, while generating a full response with minimal input may cross into academic dishonesty. Framing the conversation around intent and effort can help students think more critically about their use of these tools. Encourage transparency by requiring students to document AI interactions in their writing process. This could be a short paragraph at the end of an assignment, a comment in the document, or even a reflection prompt. Statements might include: "I used ChatGPT to help brainstorm possible counterarguments in my second paragraph" or "I asked Grammarly to help revise awkward sentences in my conclusion."

Faculty Detection vs. Student Trust

AI detection tools, like Turnitin's AI-detection feature, claim to identify AI-generated content, but these systems are not infallible. False positives can unfairly penalize students, and an overreliance on AI detection risks shifting faculty's focus from pedagogical integrity to policing students. The more instructors depend on automated AI detection, the more students may feel accused rather than trusted.

Instead of relying on AI detection, it would be more effective to redesign your assessments to make AI misuse irrelevant using the strategies described earlier in this chapter.

Balancing Automation With Human Judgment

AI efficiently automates certain assessment tasks, while human oversight remains essential for others.

AI handles the following tasks effectively:

- Grading objective assessments (multiple-choice, fill-in-the-blank, coding)
- Creating draft test questions and quiz banks from course content
- Offering preliminary feedback on mechanics, grammar, and citations
- Flagging potential plagiarism patterns

Human judgment is required for:

- Evaluating complex responses (essays, critical thinking tasks, creative work).
- Verifying whether AI-generated questions align with learning objectives.
- Understanding nuance, context, and individual perspectives.

Consider this case to understand some of these common pitfalls.

Case: AI Test Questions That Don't Measure Up

When Professor Rivera, who was teaching 20th Century Global Conflicts, faced time constraints, she asked ChatGPT to "generate 25 multiple-choice questions covering World War II." The AI quickly produced seemingly suitable questions, which she briefly reviewed before adding to her midterm.

During the exam review, students voiced frustration that the questions didn't reflect classroom learning. On closer examination, Professor Rivera realized the AI had generated factual recall questions like "In what year did the Battle of Stalingrad take place?" and "Who was the prime minister of Great Britain during World War II?" These tested only surface-level memorization rather than the critical analysis of historical perspectives and competing narratives that she emphasized in class.

For her final exam, Professor Rivera developed a more effective approach where she:

- Identified the key analytical skills and conceptual understandings she wanted to assess.
- Gave AI specific parameters like "Generate questions that require students to analyze different historical perspectives."
- Evaluated each question against criteria: "Does this assess higher-order thinking? Does it align with our class discussions?"
- Supplemented with short answer prompts requiring evidence, analysis, and argument.

Key Lesson: You need to carefully evaluate and refine generated questions so they align with learning objectives and assess higher-order thinking skills.

DESIGNING AUTHENTIC ASSESSMENTS

If you've been using the TILT framework within your assessments, you know how much clarity can impact student success. When it comes to designing authentic assessments, TILT remains a powerful tool. The difference is that for real-world or scenario-based assessments, TILT also helps students see the tangible value of their learning. They're no longer just being graded; they're tackling issues that feel real and relevant.

Structuring Assessments for Real-World Applications

Use Case Studies and Scenario-Based Assignments

Traditional assessments like multiple-choice tests and abstract essays fail to reflect real-world complexity. Instead, creating authentic assessment scenarios demands critical thinking and knowledge application. These act as mini-simulations in which students become decision-makers who must respond to multifaceted situations rather than answer theoretical questions.

For example, this prompt will generate a dilemma for an ethics course that evaluates students' critical thinking skills:

"Generate a case study for an undergraduate ethics course that presents a real-world ethical dilemma in medical decision-making. Include conflicting perspectives and key philosophical theories like utilitarianism, deontology, and virtue ethics."

Incorporate Project-Based Learning (PBL)

Project-based learning elevates ordinary assignments into dynamic projects that require research, collaboration, and creativity. Unlike isolated tasks, PBL compels students to connect multiple concepts.

Consider environmental science students who design a sustainability plan for their local community. They research, contact local agencies, survey community members, and create practical proposals.

AI can assist with solution brainstorming, proposal outlines, and data analysis. However, the core remains human-driven: data interpretation, stakeholder engagement, and navigation of real-world implementation challenges. Here is a prompt that could help design a project-based activity:

"Help me develop a sustainability project so that students connect with their community by generating research-backed action plans. Include potential environmental, economic, and social impacts, as well as feasible implementation steps."

Encourage Cross-Disciplinary Thinking

Professional problems rarely fit one domain. Pushing students to draw from multiple fields like business, psychology, computer science, and literature can help them understand the complex layers of real challenges.

For example, in psychology classes, students can analyze how behavioral science enhances workplace productivity and incorporate business concepts like organizational structure and leadership theory. AI will often suggest credible sources from both areas, though students would need to integrate these into coherent arguments themselves.

Consider this prompt:

"Write a detailed analysis of how remote work affects employee motivation and team dynamics. Consider both psychological factors (social connection, work–life boundaries, cognitive load) and business perspectives (communication structures, management strategies, performance metrics). Include examples of how these factors interact. Suggest three evidence-based recommendations that address both the psychological and business aspects of remote work productivity."

This prompt demands cross-disciplinary synthesis with practical relevance. It allows students to evaluate and expand on AI suggestions with their own insights. Such assessments reflect how professionals address challenges across fields, which aids in preparing students for modern career complexity.

Connect Course Content to Personal and Professional Experience

When students recognize connections between their coursework and their own lives, career goals, and societal responsibilities, their engagement often improves. Many students naturally transition from simply completing assignments to more actively considering how new ideas might fit into their personal worldview or professional aspirations. This is where AI becomes a useful companion rather than a substitute. If a prompt requires genuine self-reflection or real-world connections, there's little motivation for students to rely solely on AI-generated content. AI might offer a preliminary framework, but it can't recreate a student's authentic experiences, values, or emotions. When assessments feel more like stepping stones to personal or professional growth rather than hoops to jump through, students may naturally take ownership of their work when assessments are designed to foster these connections.

Connect Personal Experience and Ethical Reflection in Assignments

Assignments that demand personal reflection and ethical consideration offer unique value because AI can't replicate lived experiences or make authentic moral judgments. When students draw from their own lives or examine ethical implications, they typically engage in critical thinking that goes beyond what AI can provide.

Rather than ask "Explain this theory," consider framing questions to require personal application: "Describe when you experienced this concept in your life and connect it to the theory." Students can then apply theoretical frameworks to real situations, which requires them to process both intellectual and emotional dimensions. While AI might help organize thoughts, meaningful reflection emerges from the personal narrative.

Similarly, you could ask students to examine how AI will impact their future profession:

"How does AI currently affect your field? What ethical trade-offs exist? Consider issues like safety, job displacement, and bias in decision-making."

These prompts push students to weigh both opportunities and challenges within their career contexts. They can then interpret facts and develop balanced recommendations that consider innovation alongside ethical responsibility, which is a thought process that can't be outsourced.

AI-Assisted Assessment Models

While traditional assignments remain essential, AI tools like ChatGPT, Gemini, or Claude can enhance learning experiences. Here are three models that keep humans at the center while AI facilitates the process:

AI-Assisted Blind Review

Let students exchange work anonymously, removing bias when names aren't attached. AI can strip identifying information, distribute assignments randomly, and generate focused guiding questions about argument clarity or evidence use. Try having AI identify patterns in student feedback to spot class-wide trends you can address collectively.

AI-Scaffolded Content Creation

Encourage students to use AI in their creative process without letting it take over. They can use it during brainstorming while documenting its impact. Have students maintain AI inspiration logs noting when and why they consulted AI tools, so they practice a "use-don't-abuse" approach that sharpens the judgment employers look for.

AI-Moderated Debates

Transform classroom discussions by using AI as a debate moderator that introduces new perspectives and summarizes key points. When discussions stall, AI can pose challenging questions that force students to reconsider their assumptions. Assigning specific debate roles like proponent, opponent, and questioner encourages active participation from everyone in this real-time critical thinking exercise.

Balancing Automated and Human-Driven Assessments

As faculty redesign courses for an AI-enriched era, the pressure to create new assessments while managing a growing workload can feel daunting. The good news is that integrating modern instructional approaches augmented by, but not wholly reliant on, AI can help you strike a healthy balance. AI tools can handle certain automated tasks and free you to focus on the teaching moments that need your expertise.

Where AI works well:

- Low-stakes knowledge checks
- Grammar and structure feedback
- Rubric alignment checks
- AI-assisted brainstorming

Where human intervention is needed:

- Evaluating originality and critical thought
- Providing personalized feedback
- Interpreting ethics and intent

Balancing the Workload of Evaluating Higher-Order Assessments

One of the most significant workload challenges arises when you assign complex, open-ended tasks that demand higher-order thinking. These can be the highlight of a course but also lead to a stack of grading that seems endless. You're now facing a reality where you're expected to redesign courses and update assessments to be more AI-informed. Here are a few ways to manage that workload.

Strategies to lighten the load:

- Consider incorporating structured checkpoints where students assess each other's work or reflect on their own progress. This approach can help develop critical thinking in learners while potentially reducing the number of drafts requiring your personal evaluation.
- When feasible, staggering submission deadlines by dividing students into groups might allow you to focus your attention on smaller batches of work rather than having all major projects due simultaneously.
- For larger classes with numerous papers to review, AI tools might assist in identifying common themes or recurring questions that students are struggling with, offering opportunities to address these issues more efficiently.

More Low-Stakes Knowledge Checks, Fewer Big-Ticket Assessments

Shifting the balance toward more frequent, low-stakes assessments is a surprisingly effective way to lighten your grading load while enhancing the overall quality of student feedback. By assigning a greater number of smaller, formative tasks, online quizzes, quick polls, or brief reflection prompts, you can identify and address misconceptions early, often with minimal manual grading.

- Frequent Check-Ins
  - » A weekly online quiz that appears at the end of a module can quickly pinpoint where students are confused. These rapid-fire checks allow you to intervene long before a major exam or project is due.
- In-Class Polling
  - » Instant tools like Poll Everywhere keep students engaged in real time and provide immediate insights into their comprehension, without burying you in take-home grading.

With these short, automatically graded tasks handling the basic progress checks, you can save your energy for bigger, more meaningful assignments.

The Future of AI in Assessment

The path forward for AI looks less like an arms race against cheating and more like a collaboration that forces us to confront how we measure learning. Once, AI was simply something instructors tried to block or outsmart, a potential threat to evaluation. Now, it's emerging as a resource. It's an evolving partner rather than a silent judge. Soon enough, we may stop asking how to AI-proof our assignments and start asking how AI can push learners to dig in and become more confident in their work.

We should ask ourselves, are we capturing what students truly know and are capable of? AI might offer quicker feedback or point out oversights of a student's learning. It's up to us, the educators, to keep these assessments as honest reflections of student learning rather than just automated output.

That's why responsible experimentation with AI is key. Every institution and instructor will need to figure out what works for their students and their disciplines. That might involve a bit of trial and error. Maybe it means letting students use AI for brainstorming or adopting AI as a companion in feedback loops. Regardless of approach, our goal is to use AI to enhance assessment integrity and to never sidestep professional judgment or the effort of the learner.

With each new technological development, from ChatGPT to tools we haven't yet imagined, educators are presented with opportunities to reconsider how and why we evaluate students. AI is pushing us to think more intentionally about our designs, to shift from static checkboxes to flexible, iterative processes. In this moment, we can help shape assessments that genuinely prepare students for the world they're entering, one that will demand content knowledge, creativity, adaptability, and ethical awareness. If we embrace AI with a discerning mind and a commitment to integrity, we can create assessments that are more transparent and ultimately more human in their ability to capture what it means to learn.

DISCUSSION AND ACTIVITY

Discussion

Equitable assessment becomes more complex when students have unequal access to AI tools or varying levels of fluency with them. These disparities can shape the quality of student work, influence perceptions of competence, and widen achievement gaps. As instructors, we cannot assume that all students arrive with the same digital toolkit or the same confidence to use it.

Fair assessment in this context means evaluating students based on their understanding of course content, not their ability to navigate AI technologies. One approach is to offer multiple ways to demonstrate learning. For instance, instead of requiring students to use AI to generate a study guide, you might allow them to create one manually or use AI with guided support. This kind of choice supports different levels of comfort while keeping the academic goal intact.

Additionally, AI-based tasks should not follow a one-size-fits-all approach. Consider making them optional or offering versions that provide scaffolding. Think about how you might provide prewritten AI prompts for students who are new to the tools, while giving more open-ended options to those with experience. When possible, incorporate low-stakes practice opportunities where students can build AI fluency without pressure.

To support transparency and equity, make your expectations around AI use explicit. Clarify which tools are allowed, how they should be used, and what kind of support is available. If you suspect students lack access to reliable tools outside of class, consider building in-class time for them to explore and practice with institutional resources if available.

Fairness in AI-enhanced assessment involves adapting your approach so that the evaluation reflects what you want students to learn, not how tech-savvy they are in reaching those goals.

I invite you to think about these two reflection questions:

- How might we balance encouraging AI literacy while keeping assessment focused on course content rather than technological proficiency?
- In what ways can instructors create assessment options that accommodate different levels of AI access and experience without compromising academic standards?

Designing for Process Over Product

Consider shifting your assessment design to highlight the steps students take, not just what they create. Their approach to research, decision-making, and adaptation matters more than ever now. This emphasis on process discourages shortcuts and builds the habits of reflection and iteration that extend beyond the classroom.

To redesign assessments with this in mind, build in multiple checkpoints that allow students to demonstrate progress over time. This helps them slow down, receive feedback along the way, and focus on skill-building rather than cramming.

Use prompts and tools that make thinking visible. Ask students to write short process reflections after they complete a milestone, explaining what they changed and why. Consider requiring revision memos with each draft to track how their understanding evolved.

AI can support this kind of design. Students might use AI tools to brainstorm, gather examples, or clarify concepts early in the process but then document how that input shaped their next steps. Ask them to describe their interactions with AI and explain how they evaluated its usefulness. These small moments of metacognition are just as valuable as the finished product. When we prioritize the process, we reinforce the value of learning over performance. We create more meaningful, honest assessments that give students room to grow.

Please consider these two reflection questions:

- How might focusing on process rather than product change a student's relationship with their personal learning and experience with AI tools?
- What specific checkpoints or reflective practices in your subject areas could help students value their learning journey while still maintaining high standards for their final work?

Activity

Purpose

Redesign an existing assessment to incorporate AI responsibly while helping students use AI appropriately. Applying AI-informed design principles alongside the TILT framework can result in clearer, fairer assessments aligned with meaningful learning outcomes.

Task

1. **Choose an Assessment to Potentially Redesign**
   » Select an existing assessment where AI could assist with feedback, question generation, or shift focus to learning process.

2. **Apply AI-Informed Design Principles**
   » *Fairness*: Address advantages from unequal AI access.
   » *Process Focus*: Emphasize drafting, peer review, and reflection; consider requiring AI-use statements.
   » *Authenticity*: Testing questions with AI can help identify prompts that might be too easily handled and could benefit from redesign.
3. **Apply TILT Framework**
   » *Purpose*: Connect to learning goals.
   » *Task*: Clarify AI use expectations.
   » *Criteria*: Define quality work and AI evaluation standards.
4. **Example**
   » *Before*: Write a five-page essay on the causes of the French Revolution.
   » *After*: Write a five-page essay on the causes of the French Revolution. You may use AI for outlines and grammar, but all historical analysis must be your own. Submit an AI-use statement. Grading based on historical accuracy, analysis depth, and argument clarity.

CHAPTER 6

Upholding Academic Integrity

Strategies to Combat Cheating in the AI Era

THE CHALLENGES OF ACADEMIC INTEGRITY

Introduction

I give a lot of talks to institutions and departments that are just starting to reckon with AI's impact on education. There's a slide I use in these presentations where I connect critical thinking to academic integrity. It's simple—just a few words—but they always land. I say "The days of the five-paragraph essay are over." Faculty usually shift in their seats when I say it. Some nod; others look skeptical. Then I follow up: "If you send your students off to write a one-page paper on what they learned from your lecture, then it's a wrap." At that moment, you can see the realization settle in. The way we've structured assessments for decades is fundamentally incompatible with the reality of generative AI. This isn't a challenge; it's an opportunity.

AI has arrived in education with force. We're in the middle of a seismic shift, one that compels us to rethink what we assign and how we assess learning. The traditional safeguards against cheating weren't built for a world where students can generate a polished essay or solve equations in seconds with the right prompt. The goalposts have moved, and faculty are scrambling to adapt. Right now, we are living in the "Wild West" of AI policies. Some institutions are attempting to push ahead with strict policies banning AI. Others are integrating AI into coursework and treating it like any other academic tool. And then there are departments where every individual faculty member makes their own call. The result? A chaotic patchwork of rules, expectations, and student confusion. In my conversations with faculty and leadership across multiple institutions, I've encountered a recurring theme: Many want a blanket policy, a simple, universal rule that dictates AI's place in education. But there's no single policy that can address the needs of every discipline, department, and course. A broad institutional policy can set a foundation, but at the end of the day, AI policies need to be flexible enough to account for the needs of different fields. That means shifting the conversation from "Should we allow AI?" to "How do we guide students in using AI responsibly?"

I saw this tension play out firsthand in a faculty workshop I led. A math professor was skeptical about AI's capabilities. He wondered out loud, "Could AI even complete my calculus test?" Curious, I took a picture of his screen and uploaded it to ChatGPT. Within seconds, the AI worked through the problems, explaining each step. It all happens on the projector. The room fell silent as the solution unfolded in real time.

This is the landscape we're navigating. AI is here, and it's forcing us to rethink what academic integrity means in a world where knowledge production is no longer solely a human endeavor. Instead of fighting AI or banning it outright, our role as educators is to equip students with the critical thinking skills necessary to use these tools with integrity.

How AI Can Be Misused for Cheating

By now, it's no secret that AI can generate essays, write code, and solve complex problems for us. If a student wants to submit an assignment they didn't actually write, they don't need to steal from Wikipedia, subscribe to Chegg (a subscription-based service that provides textbook solutions and homework help), or buy a prewritten paper from a laid-off adjunct professor. With just a few well-crafted prompts, they can generate original work that doesn't show up in traditional plagiarism checks. The tools meant to catch academic dishonesty are struggling to keep up, and generative AI isn't slowing down anytime soon.

But the problem extends far beyond text generation. AI vision tools can now scan and solve math and physics problems directly from a screenshot. Used correctly, this is an incredible tool for learning. Our students can check their work on demand and analyze different solution methods 24 hours a day without the need to make an appointment with a tutor or wait for a reply from an instructor. But let's be real: This is the shortcut through critical thinking I like to talk about. It makes it incredibly easy to bypass learning altogether. Instead of working through problems, students can simply submit AI-generated answers as their own, and then it's up to us to discern if the student demonstrated their knowledge.

And then there's AI paraphrasing, a rapidly growing concern in the fight against plagiarism. AI tools can take an existing essay, rewrite it in new words, and make it practically unrecognizable to detection software. Many plagiarism checkers rely on exact wording matches to flag unoriginal work, but AI-generated paraphrasing sidesteps these systems without breaking a sweat. This means that even if students aren't copying directly from a source, they can still submit work that isn't truly their own, while making it nearly impossible for instructors to prove otherwise.

This is where the landscape of academic integrity is shifting. It's not about catching copied-and-pasted work anymore. AI is making it easier than ever to blur the lines between assistance and dishonesty, and the responsibility falls on us as educators to recognize these new challenges and adapt accordingly.

The Detection Dilemma

AI detection tools have become a hot topic in academic integrity discussions, but the truth is that they tend to be flawed. Institutions have rushed to adopt software designed to catch AI-generated writing, yet these tools are far from reliable. They produce false positives that unfairly accuse students of using AI when they haven't and generate false negatives that allow AI-generated work to slip through undetected. The technology meant to safeguard academic honesty is, ironically, creating new ethical concerns of its own.

One of the biggest issues with AI detection is that it frequently misidentifies well-structured, high-quality student work as AI-generated. A student who writes with clarity, coherence, and strong organization, hallmarks of good writing, may find themselves flagged simply because their work is too polished. This problem is even worse for non-native English speakers. Research from Stanford has shown that AI detectors disproportionately classify their writing as AI-generated, largely because these systems rely on perplexity scores, which measure sentence complexity and predictability (Myers, 2023). The result? A bias that unfairly penalizes students whose first language isn't English, reinforcing systemic disadvantages rather than addressing actual misconduct.

To make matters worse, AI technology is evolving too quickly for detection tools to keep pace. OpenAI itself acknowledges that detecting AI-generated text is unreliable, as even small edits to AI-produced work can evade detection (OpenAI, n.d.). The arms race between AI text generators and detection software is one that detection tools are consistently losing. As new models become more sophisticated, the ability to distinguish between human and AI writing becomes even murkier.

This leads to a larger question: Where do we draw the line between AI assistance and dishonesty? A student who uses AI to generate a reading response or discussion post based on course materials isn't the same as one who submits an AI-generated essay verbatim, yet AI detection tools don't operate with such nuance. We are now confronting cases that challenge traditional notions of cheating. Is it unethical if a student uses AI to generate study guides or outlines but writes the final submission themselves? What about a student who wrote an original paper but uses AI to rephrase sentences to improve readability? The rigid frameworks of AI detection tools fail to account for the context, reducing complex academic questions to binary verdicts of "cheating" or "not cheating."

The unreliability of AI detection means that institutions relying on these tools as the sole measure of academic integrity are creating more problems than they're solving. A more balanced approach is needed, one that incorporates human oversight, clear AI usage policies, and an understanding that AI is now a fundamental part of the learning process. Instead of playing an endless game of cat and mouse with detection software, you'll get further ahead by guiding students to use AI responsibly.

Gray Areas: AI Use That Sparks Debate

At what point does using AI transition from academic support to academic dishonesty? The boundaries are murky, and students often don't realize how easily AI tools can overstep their intended role. Even if a student only asks for an outline, many AI systems will generate full paragraphs, suggest key arguments, or even provide citations, offering more than was requested. AI is designed to be helpful, which often means providing more than the student intended to use. This creates a subtle but significant dilemma: at what point does assistance become authorship?

As AI tools become more sophisticated and accessible, where should we draw the line with students? While some AI applications function as productivity enhancers, helping students organize ideas or debug code, others generate substantial portions of work with minimal input. The challenge lies in determining when AI serves as a learning aid versus when it becomes a substitute for independent thought. As institutions navigate these evolving dilemmas, real-world examples highlight the nuanced ethical questions surrounding AI use in academia.

John: AI in Programming Assignments

John, a computer science major, is working on a machine learning algorithm for image recognition. Throughout the project, he uses an AI coding assistant to debug his code, suggest more efficient algorithms, and explain complex concepts. His final submission is a blend of his original work and AI-suggested improvements. While he documents his use of AI in his project notes, he doesn't explicitly disclose it in his final submission, believing the final product represents his own understanding and effort.

During a code review, a classmate recognizes some coding patterns typical of an AI assistant and raises the issue. This sparks a classroom debate: Should AI-generated code be treated differently from human-authored work, even when used as an aid? What guidelines should the department establish for AI use in programming courses when they know more employers will be implementing AI coding assistants?

Emma: AI for Research and Writing

Emma, a graduate student in environmental science, is writing a research paper on the economic impacts of climate change. She uses AI to summarize academic papers, generate an outline, and suggest arguments. However, she spends weeks writing the final paper herself, incorporating additional research and analysis. She cites all her sources but doesn't disclose her use of AI for organization and brainstorming.

Emma's paper is selected for publication in a student journal, and during the editing process, she is asked about her research methodology. This raises an important question: Should AI be disclosed in research if it only contributed to the organizational process? Would disclosure change how her work is perceived?

Alex: AI in Mathematical Problem Solving

Alex, a mathematics major, is completing a take-home exam for an advanced calculus course. After struggling with a difficult integration problem for hours, she turns to an AI-powered math solver. Instead of copying the answer, she studies the solution and then works through the problem independently, making sure she understands each step before writing it out in her own words and notation.

Her department is divided on the issue. Some faculty believe that AI-powered math solvers are an essential modern tool, while others argue they undermine fundamental problem-solving skills. This raises the question: Should AI-powered math solvers be integrated into the curriculum, or do they compromise academic integrity? How can the department strike a balance between traditional mathematical training and AI-assisted learning?

Classroom Debates: Defining Ethical AI Use

AI's role in education isn't just a policy issue for faculty, it's a conversation that students need to be part of. These scenarios can serve as a foundation for classroom debates where students actively define what they consider ethical AI use.

- Where should institutions draw the line between acceptable AI assistance and academic shortcuts?
- Should students be required to disclose their use of AI in coursework, even if it only played a minor role?
- Does AI usage enhance learning, or does it create an overreliance on technology?

By having these open discussions, you can develop clearer guidelines that reflect the realities of AI in education while also helping students take an active role in shaping ethical academic practices.

STRATEGIES FOR MAINTAINING INTEGRITY

Clarifying AI Expectations in Assessments

As we explored in Chapter 5, you already know the ways AI is reshaping assessment and the importance of designing assignments that emphasize process over product. We've discussed why AI-proofing assessments is a losing battle and why transparency in AI use should be a core principle. In this section, we'll take those ideas a step further, focusing on how to implement clear AI policies within assessments to reinforce academic integrity without stifling innovation.

Set Clear Boundaries on AI Use

Rather than leaving students to guess when and how AI can be used, we should be explicit. If AI is allowed for brainstorming but not for drafting entire assignments, state that directly. If students can use AI to refine their writing but not to create content from scratch, clarify those expectations up front. Instead of vague "don't use AI to cheat" statements, try to provide specific guidelines:

- **Allowed:** Using AI to summarize research articles, generate outlines, or check grammar.
- **Not Allowed:** Submitting AI-generated responses without revision, using AI to complete problem-solving exercises, or relying on AI to construct original arguments without critical engagement.

To support accountability, students could be asked to document their AI use. A brief AI Use Statement accompanying each assignment can encourage reflection and transparency. This not only encourages students to engage responsibly with AI but also helps them develop metacognitive awareness about their learning process.

Reinforce the Importance of Process, Not Just Product

One of the more effective ways to prevent students from submitting AI-generated work without critical engagement is to require them to show their thinking. By structuring assessments to emphasize the journey rather than just the final product, we can make tools like ChatGPT an aid rather than a shortcut.

Consider these approaches:

- **Annotated Drafts:** Students submit early drafts with AI-generated content clearly marked and revisions explained.
- **Reflection Questions:** Ask students to articulate their reasoning process, evaluate AI-generated suggestions, and describe the decision-making behind their final submission.
- **Step-by-Step Explanations:** In problem-solving tasks, require students to document their thought process rather than presenting only a final answer.

Embedding transparency and reflection into assignments allows you to move AI from being a replacement tool to a learning amplifier.

Recognizing AI Influence in Student Work

AI-generated writing isn't always easy to spot, but sometimes, you just know when something feels . . . off. Humans are fantastic at pattern recognition, and while AI is constantly evolving, there are still a few tells that can indicate when a piece of writing may not be entirely human-driven. That said, there are no foolproof methods. Language is weird, flexible, and unpredictable. It's much like AI itself. What seems like a clear giveaway today might not hold up tomorrow as this technology advances. Still, keeping an eye on key markers can help you make informed evaluations.

Identifying Work That Feels Too Advanced or Inconsistent

One of the first red flags is when a student's work suddenly shifts in quality, either improving drastically overnight or displaying inconsistencies within the same piece. If a student who has historically struggled with organization and clarity submits an essay that reads like a polished academic article, it's worth a closer look. Likewise, if an assignment starts with one writing style and suddenly shifts to another mid-paragraph, AI could be at play.

Another telltale sign appears in problem-solving assignments, particularly in subjects like mathematics, physics, and computer science. If a student who previously demonstrated only a basic grasp of algebra suddenly submits a calculus-based solution to a problem that didn't require it, or if a physics answer includes derivations and notations that are beyond the course level, you should take a closer look. Similarly, in coding assignments, a student who struggled with writing simple loops might suddenly submit an optimized algorithm using advanced data structures that haven't been covered in class. In humanities or social sciences, students might reference niche theoretical frameworks or cite obscure academic sources that they are unlikely to have encountered without external guidance. When solutions showcase methodologies or insights that align more with advanced or graduate-level coursework than the current curriculum, it's worth investigating how the student arrived at their answer.

When Writing Lacks a Personal Voice or Discipline-Specific Nuance

Good writing carries a fingerprint. It reflects personality, experience, and a certain familiarity with a subject. AI-generated text, on the other hand, often lacks this distinctiveness. It might be grammatically correct but devoid of individuality, making it feel generic or oddly detached from the topic.

Discipline-specific writing also has nuances in its terminology, expected structures, and common ways ideas are presented. AI sometimes gets these wrong, producing writing that sounds competent on the surface but misuses key concepts or applies them in a way that doesn't align with how experts in the field would naturally communicate.

Specific AI Giveaways (for Now)

While AI is getting better at mimicking human writing, it still has quirks. The following indicators aren't foolproof, but they can serve as general guidance. This is particularly the case for longer, information-driven texts rather than short-form or highly stylized writing.

- **Unnatural Phrasing and Awkward Transitions**
    - » **The Tell:** Sentences that feel off, maybe too stiff, too formal, or strangely worded. Transitions between ideas might be abrupt or nonsensical. AI struggles with making writing flow in a way that feels natural and conversational.
- **Excessive Formality or a Formulaic Structure**
    - » **The Tell:** Text that follows a predictable pattern, using rigid grammatical structures and sticking too closely to basic rules. It may also lack the natural variety of tone, rhythm, and word choice that human writing typically includes.
- **Lack of Definitive Judgments or Personal Opinions**
    - » **The Tell:** AI-generated text tends to hedge a lot. It presents multiple perspectives without taking a strong stance, often sounding like a Wikipedia summary rather than an actual argument. If an assignment avoids personal reflection or decisive conclusions when they would be expected, it may be a sign of AI involvement.
- **Overuse of Clichés or Generic Language**
    - » **The Tell:** ChatGPT loves clichés and generic phrasing. It will often use broad, nonspecific statements instead of concrete, unique descriptions. If a paper is filled with phrases like "in today's fast-paced world" or "staying ahead of the curve is crucial," that could be a sign of AI-generated fluff.

Faculty Strategies for AI-Informed Engagement with Students

How faculty respond when students use AI to assist with their work can either foster a culture of learning or create an atmosphere of unnecessary conflict. The goal isn't to catch and punish; rather, it's to guide students toward effective use of artificial intelligence in their academic journey. That starts with shifting the focus from suspicion to conversation.

Engage in Conversations Rather Than Accusations

The quickest way to erode trust in the classroom is to make sweeping claims about how easily AI-generated work can be detected. While there are some indicators, no method is foolproof. Approaching a student with an accusatory tone, especially if you can't be certain, can put them on the defensive and damage the instructor–student relationship. Instead, engage in a dialogue. If you notice inconsistencies in a student's work, ask them to walk you through their thought process. How did they arrive at their conclusions? What sources did they use? By making the conversation about learning rather than blame, you create an environment where students are more likely to be honest and reflective about their use of AI tools.

Encourage Students to Disclose AI Use

Rather than treating AI use as a problem, try to normalize discussions around it. Build AI disclosure into your assignments by asking students to submit an AI Use Statement with their work. These statements typically include:

- **Tool Identification**
    - » *Name of the AI Tool/Platform*
    - » *Version or Access Method*: If relevant (e.g., ChatGPT-4o vs. ChatGPT-o1 or a specific plugin/extension).
- **Purpose of Use**
    - » *Description of the Task*: Ask students to describe what they used the AI tool for.
    - » *Extent of AI Assistance*: Students should clarify if AI merely provided grammatical suggestions, offered general feedback, or contributed larger sections of text or code.
- **Dates/Timeline of AI Interaction**
    - » *When and How Often*: Ask students to note when in their process they used AI (beginning for idea generation, midway for editing, or final check for proofreading) and how frequently (one-time query vs. multiple iterations).
- **Verification and Editing**
    - » *Student's Own Review*: Encourage students to explain how they verified, validated, or edited AI-generated content.
    - » *Quality Control*: Did they fact-check, compare AI outputs to original sources, or cross-reference any suggestions?
- **Reflection on the AI's Role**
    - » *Learning Reflection*: Ask them to comment on how the AI's input shaped their thinking, writing, or problem-solving approach.
    - » *Limitations Acknowledgment*: Encourage honesty about errors or limitations of AI output and how they addressed them.
- **Statement of Responsibility**
    - » *Student Accountability*: Students should affirm that they take responsibility for the final work's content, regardless of the AI's involvement.
    - » *Academic Integrity Considerations*: Remind students that while AI can assist, the work must meet the course's integrity standards. Plagiarism or misrepresentation remains the student's responsibility.

Emphasize Learning Over Punitive Measures

Proving AI use beyond a doubt is difficult. Instead of relying on detection tools that may flag false positives, consider shifting your approach. If a student's work raises concerns, use it as an opportunity to redirect rather than reprimand.

- Ask the student to elaborate on their work in a follow-up discussion or reflection.
- Integrating more process-based assessments—such as in-class drafts, revisions, or oral explanations of written work—can provide insights into student learning. You might discover that including additional presentations with major assignments helps verify student understanding.
- Focusing on skill development rather than punishment tends to be more effective in the long run. When students appear to overrely on AI, offering guidance to help them build the skills needed for more independent work supports their academic growth.

By framing AI use as a learning opportunity rather than a disciplinary issue, you can reinforce academic integrity while keeping the focus where it belongs. More than anything, we want to make sure we never erode the trust between you and your students.

DEVELOPING EFFECTIVE AI POLICIES

Why Blanket AI Policies Fail

As institutions wrestle with the integration of AI into classrooms, there is a temptation to create universal policies that apply across all courses and disciplines. While this approach is well-intentioned, it often fails in practice. The effectiveness of these kinds of policies depends on their adaptability to specific academic contexts. A one-size-fits-all policy risks either being too restrictive and stifling the benefits of AI, or too permissive, which fails to set boundaries. Instead, your guidelines should be created to align with the needs of each faculty member as they know their learning objectives and assessment methods for their courses.

No two courses are identical. Their academic integrity expectations shouldn't be either. A blanket policy regarding AI use applied to every discipline ignores the different needs of various subjects. It would be reasonable to expect an instructor leading a writing course to want to prohibit AI use in their course, while a data science course will need to educate students in its use for statistical modeling.

Tailoring these policies helps make sure that technology is used to enhance learning rather than diminish essential skill development.

The Struggle With Inconsistent Guidelines

Students are already burdened with navigating a growing web of academic expectations. The introduction of AI has only added to this challenge. When different instructors or departments implement conflicting rules, it creates confusion and increases the risk of unintentional violations. Each student may have some instructors allowing its use and others who ban it. All the while, these students are also dealing with a sea of gray when it comes to these expectations.

To mitigate this, institutions should establish clear guidelines that instructors can adapt based on the needs of their course. Try to make it a priority to communicate your specific expectations regarding the use of artificial intelligence at the beginning of each term, and reinforce it in writing via your syllabus and in your initial classroom discussions. This consistency is going to allow your students to approach these tools with confidence knowing what is and isn't acceptable in each of their learning environments.

It's helpful for students to understand that they'll likely encounter different policies at various points in their academic careers. Just as citation styles or group work vary by discipline, using AI will be governed by different standards set by the instructor for each course. Instructors should actively encourage students to ask questions when expectations are unclear or seem inconsistent. Creating space for these conversations helps prevent confusion and reinforces a classroom culture where dialogue around AI use is open and ongoing.

The Need for Discipline-Specific Approaches

The impact and application of this technology is going to vary widely across various disciplines, making it essential to craft guidelines that reflect the specific needs of each field. Below are examples of how AI policies can be structured in some of the most common university subjects.

- **Mathematics:** Tools like Wolfram Alpha will solve equations near instantaneously, but students still need to understand the underlying concepts. Consider permitting AI to check solutions but not for completing homework without showing the work. Think about developing policies that require students to submit handwritten calculations alongside any AI assistance they receive.
- **Business:** In business courses, the likely uses of AI will be centered around data analysis, market research, and case study work. Your policies should reflect the real-world AI application of developing initial drafts of reports and presentations with a requirement that students verify the facts and

contribute human insights. It's increasingly likely that this process reflects how companies will expect employees to use this technology, and students should be prepared to leverage it effectively.

- **Health Sciences:** Given the importance of accuracy in medical education, consider tightly regulating AI use. It can assist with literature reviews and summarizing research, but consider not allowing students to use it for things like clinical assessments or patient diagnosis unless it's explicitly needed for a specific application. Your policy should emphasize critical evaluation of any content generated by these systems.
- **Computer Science:** Many applications, like GitHub Copilot, include AI code development features, yet students still need to develop their own programming skills. Think about policies that allow them to learn how to use these features effectively, so they learn marketable skills in the modern programming environment. Maybe AI is allowed to debug code or generate templates, but your assignments require students to explain AI contributions to the comments or a reflection piece.

When developing discipline-specific AI policies, the TPACK framework provides valuable structure. Different fields have unique relationships among content, teaching methods, and how technology like AI fits into authentic learning. These contextual decisions reflect the TPACK principle that effective technology integration always considers both pedagogical goals and subject matter needs.

The goal of these policies should not be to ban or restrict innovation but to guide AI use in ways that enhance learning rather than replace essential skills students will need. By tailoring guidelines to individual courses and disciplines, institutions will then be able to provide clarity for students while maintaining the integrity of their academic programs.

Providing Transparency on Permitted and Restricted Use

As AI becomes more embedded in academic work, you will need to provide clarity on when and how students can use these tools. Ambiguous policies create confusion and can lead to either misuse or missed opportunities. The solution? Clearly defined boundaries.

Clarity on Boundaries

Students shouldn't have to guess whether they are allowed to use ChatGPT for a given assignment. The policy you've developed should explicitly outline which functions are permitted and which are not. What if you'd like to allow students to use AI to brainstorm or refine their grammar but not generate any actual writing for their essay? If you haven't made that clear, your students will end up guessing. A policy with clear, concise expectations removes uncertainty and helps your students make informed decisions about how they engage with AI systems.

It's not enough to simply list dos and don'ts; your students will benefit from real-world scenarios illustrating what appropriate use looks like. Consider incorporating the following examples into your syllabus:

- *Appropriate Use*: You can use AI to generate an initial topic idea for your research paper, then you refine those ideas and write your own argument.
- *Inappropriate Use:* Uploading the assignment prompt into ChatGPT, then copying the generated output and submitting it as your own work.

These scenarios may seem straightforward, but by offering examples, you give students a clearer understanding of your expectations and boundaries.

Guide Students Rather Than Punish Ambiguity

A well-designed AI policy should not function as a trap. Instead of approaching AI use from a strictly punitive perspective, your policies should focus on educating students about ethical and responsible integration of AI into their work.

Rather than leading with restrictions, take an educational approach. AI literacy is now a fundamental skill, and students should be encouraged to engage with these tools in a way that prepares them for the evolving role it plays in society. By teaching students how to integrate AI responsibly, we prepare them for professional environments where this technology is becoming the standard.

Students will inevitably make mistakes. Instead of harsh penalties for first-time missteps, think about how to establish mechanisms for continuous feedback. Consider including a requirement to submit AI-use statements alongside assignments. Give students an opportunity to detail what they used AI for and how it shaped their work.

Communicating AI Policies Clearly

AI is here to stay, and students are already using it. Instead of ignoring or fearing it, why not set the tone from day one with an open conversation? Clearly defining the role of AI in your course creates a shared understanding and avoids confusion down the line. The key is to be proactive, transparent, and approachable.

Syllabus and First-Day Discussion

Your syllabus is the perfect place to introduce AI guidelines. Setting clear expectations from the start helps your students understand what you expect of them. Embedding your AI policy in the course syllabus guarantees that they are documented, consistent, and easily accessible. Just make sure your policies aren't buried in the fine print. They should be prominent and easy to reference. Clearly outline:

- Which AI tools and functions are permitted (e.g., using ChatGPT for brainstorming ideas, Grammarly for grammar refinement, or Perplexity for sourcing background information).
- Which uses are prohibited (e.g., AI-generated essays, automated problem solving).
- Whether and how students should disclose AI use in their work.

Example Syllabus Language

AI tools like ChatGPT may be used for brainstorming and grammar checks, but all written work must be your own. If your work was AI-assisted, you must include an AI Use Statement detailing how the tool was used. For example:

- I used ChatGPT to brainstorm topic ideas for this paper. All research, writing, and analysis were completed independently.
- I used an AI tool to revise grammar and sentence structure in my first draft. The content and ideas are my own.
- I used an AI tool to check my calculations and review the steps for solving one of the problems. All final answers and written explanations are my own.

Policies are more effective when students understand their rationale. Instead of simply enforcing rules, encourage open conversations. Ask students to reflect on the benefits and limitations of AI, its ethical implications, and how it applies to their field of study.

Dedicate time on the first day of class to discuss these policies. Rather than only reading policy language aloud, you might invite students to share which tools they've used before. This can spark engagement and give you a better sense of their familiarity with the technology and which tools are gaining traction.

- **Example Icebreaker:** "Before we get into today's material, I want to hear from you. Who here has used an AI tool like ChatGPT? What did you use it for? Was it helpful?"

Something like this opens the door to have a dialogue about your policies and how you expect students to use these tools responsibly.

Keep Your Policies Consistent

Inconsistency between how you write about the policy in your syllabus and how it's talked about in class can lead to confusion. If your syllabus states that AI use requires citation, but you tell students informally that "it's fine as long as you don't overdo it," they'll be left guessing what the actual rule is.

To maintain clarity:

- Policies are most effective when they align with university guidelines, where available.
- Maintaining consistent language across lectures, assignments, and your syllabus helps reduce confusion and reinforces expectations for students.
- Offering examples that illustrate appropriate AI use can give students clearer guidance about your expectations.

As a good rule of thumb, if students leave your class wondering whether they'll get in trouble for using AI, your policy isn't clear enough. Consider checking in through informal student feedback, mid-semester reflections, or brief anonymous surveys to gauge whether expectations around AI use are understood.

Ongoing Reinforcement

A one-time mention isn't enough. As these tools continue to evolve, your students may forget initial guidelines or misunderstand acceptable use. Revisiting AI policies at key points in the semester, such as before major assignments or exams, helps reinforce expectations when students might be most tempted to take shortcuts. It might get tempting to get some help from ChatGPT when deadlines get tighter.

So, before you assign a research paper, remind students: "You can use AI to help generate ideas or organize your thoughts, but the analysis needs to be your own. If you're unsure whether a tool's use is appropriate, ask before submitting."

Now, you're creating an environment where students feel confident navigating AI use and comfortable asking you for clarification when they don't.

Updates and Adaptive Review

This technology is evolving every day, and policies that are effective today may need adjustments next semester. Schedule periodic reviews to make sure your guidelines remain relevant and practical. Gather anonymous feedback from students to understand their challenges and insights regarding how they've been using it.

Also, these policies shouldn't be crafted in a vacuum. It can be helpful to involve colleagues and students in policy revisions to keep your guidelines realistic, comprehensive, and aligned with your department or program's expectations. Collaborating across disciplines may also lead to more thoughtful policies that reflect insights and implications from other fields. If your class is a general education requirement that supports majors in fields like computer science, health sciences, or education, you'll want to be thoughtful about how your policies set the tone for students entering those programs. In these cases, students may benefit from more consistent expectations across courses, especially when it comes to foundational skills like writing, research, or responsible AI use. While some variation is necessary across disciplines, identifying shared principles can help reduce confusion and support academic integrity across the curriculum.

CONVERSATIONS ABOUT MISUSE

Building a Culture of Integrity

When talking to students about AI use, we want to avoid setting traps or playing detective and move toward building a classroom culture where integrity is the norm. Students need to understand that these tools are not a shortcut and that responsible use is a skill they'll need long after they leave your course. The key isn't just in setting rules but in fostering a mindset where ethical engagement feels like the obvious, natural choice.

Fostering a Growth Mindset With AI

Try not to think about AI tools as an enemy of learning. In fact, AI can be a powerful tool for developing critical thinking. But that requires a shift in how students see their own growth. If they believe the goal of an assignment is just to submit something, anything, that checks the required boxes, AI will feel like a tempting shortcut. If instead they understand that the real goal is to expand their thinking, it becomes a tool for curiosity rather than an ejection cord they can pull when there's trouble.

One way to reinforce this is by framing assignments as opportunities to build skills rather than produce polished work.

- Invite students to create an AI-assisted draft and then revise it extensively, noting what the AI missed and how they improved the work.
- Suggest a comparison between their own writing and an AI-generated response, with attention to the strengths and limitations of each.
- *Prompt reflection*: In what ways did AI shape their process? Did it support deeper thinking, or did it shift their engagement with the material?

Highlight the Long-Term Consequences

Misuse also leads to self-sabotage. Students who rely too much on AI may get by in the short term, but eventually, the gaps in their understanding will catch up with them.

- In advanced courses, instructors expect students to build on prior knowledge. A student who let ChatGPT do all the heavy lifting in early classes might find themselves struggling in classes that require understanding of more advanced topics or hands-on skills.
- Employers want critical thinkers who can ask the right questions and synthesize complex information, not just generate content. AI won't do that for them.
- Developing real expertise takes effort. When students skip the hard work, they're cutting corners and depriving themselves of the skills and confidence they'll need beyond the classroom.

Helping students make these connections within the bigger picture is essential. If they understand that genuine learning can't be outsourced, they're more likely to make better choices.

Teaching Responsible AI Engagement as a Critical Skill

AI will continue to play an expanding role in education, and the need for ethical decision-making will remain just as important. Instead of banning AI entirely, consider guiding students on how to use it thoughtfully and responsibly. That means setting clear expectations, modeling best practices, and making ethical use a visible part of academic and professional discussions.

If students see AI as an off-limits, shadowy tool, they'll be more likely to use it dishonestly. Instead, try to normalize responsible use by demonstrating it yourself:

- Show students how AI can be used transparently in research, writing, and problem solving.
  - » You might ask students to begin a research paper by using AI to generate a draft or summary. From there, they can review the output, identify any inaccuracies, and enhance the content by adding their own insights.
- Incorporate AI-generated content into lessons, then critique it together. What does it get right? Where does it fall short?
  - » Consider generating an AI-written essay in class and having students work in groups to explore its strengths and limitations. Together, discuss where human input might be needed to enhance coherence, depth, or analysis.
- Model proper citation and disclosure. APA and MLA both offer guidelines on citing AI-generated content; use them. Demonstrate this by incorporating it into an assignment and walking students through the citation process.

Link Ethical Use to Professional Standards

Ethical use is both an academic issue and a professional one. Every field is grappling with how to incorporate AI responsibly into its workflows and products. Future journalists will need to verify facts. Engineers will need to verify that models perform calculations correctly. Health care professionals will have to interpret diagnostics responsibly and with a critical eye. The students in your classroom today will soon be making these decisions in the workplace.

Helping students connect classroom integrity to real-world responsibility strengthens the message. Ethical use moves beyond just following the rules and helps students develop habits of honesty and discernment that will serve them long after graduation.

Conversations about AI misuse shouldn't feel like policing. They should feel like coaching, helping students make informed choices because they understand the value of learning, not just out of fear of getting caught. By building a culture of integrity, we're better positioned to prevent misconduct and prepare students for a future where knowing how to use AI responsibly will be just as important as knowing how to use it at all.

Navigating Tough Conversations About AI Misuse

The goal of these conversations is to understand students' thinking and guide them toward ethical choices. If we approach with curiosity, we open the door for honest dialogue and learning.

Acknowledge Uncertainty

You can't be 100% certain that a student used AI inappropriately. Often, leading with accusations will backfire, breaking trust and making your student less likely to work with you earnestly. Instead, frame concerns as questions:

- "I'm noticing some new patterns in your writing. Can you walk me through how you arrived at this work?"
- "Your recent submissions have improved significantly. That's great! What strategies have you been using to develop your writing?"

This gives students the opportunity to explain their process, acknowledge their challenges, and, if needed, recognize any missteps without feeling attacked.

Focus on Understanding

Instead of making the conversation solely about policy violations, try to use it as a moment to understand what might have driven the student's choices. Was it a time crunch? A misunderstanding of course expectations? External pressures? Many students who misuse AI do it not out of dishonesty but out of desperation or confusion.

Modern students are balancing an increasing number of stressors. They're facing academic pressures, work obligations, and personal challenges. You may also be noticing more nontraditional learners in your classroom. These students are juggling full-time jobs, caregiving responsibilities, or returning to school after years away. The temptation to lean on AI tools can be even stronger. Recognizing these factors allows for a more empathetic approach and helps students to build better time management and study habits rather than defaulting to shortcuts that hinder their long-term learning.

By focusing on the why, you can work together to find better strategies for managing their workload and using AI responsibly in the future. More importantly, it reinforces that you care about their learning, not just their compliance.

Building Trust in Difficult Conversations

Encourage Verbal Defense

A simple way to assess a student's understanding of their work is to ask them to walk you through their process:

- "Walk me through how you developed this thesis statement."
- "What challenges did you encounter while writing this section?"
- "Show me your drafts or outline that led to this final version."

Look for hesitation, vague responses, or inability to explain specific decisions. A student who genuinely created the work can typically discuss their thinking, including false starts and revisions.

- **Create a Learning-Focused Environment**
  - » Begin with curiosity rather than accusation.
    - "I'd like to understand your approach to this assignment."
  - » Emphasize growth over punishment.
    - "My goal is to help you develop genuine academic skills."
  - » Use physical evidence when possible.
    - Ask to see research notes, draft versions, or annotation methods.
- **Specific Intervention Strategies**
  - » Consider using a brief verbal quiz to get a sense of students' understanding.
  - » You might ask students to write a quick summary of key arguments without using notes or reference materials.

    - » Invite them to revise a section of their work during class while walking through the reasoning behind their changes.
- **Constructive Next Steps**
    - » Consider offering a revision opportunity with guidance to help students build on their work.
    - » Share resources that support authentic research and writing practices.
    - » Follow up with check-ins that encourage progress and keep students on track.

Identify Gaps

If a student is using terminology, strategies, or advanced concepts that weren't covered in class, ask them about it:

- "This section introduces an advanced concept we haven't discussed yet. Can you explain how you arrived at this analysis?"
- "You solved this problem using a method I didn't cover in class."
- "You reference a study we didn't cover; what led you to that source?"

This encourages students to think about their own work and provides a chance to assess whether their engagement with AI has been educational or purely generative.

Discuss Motivations

Many students don't see AI as cheating; they see it as a time-saver. Help them reflect on how their choices impact their learning:

- "What led you to use AI in this assignment?"
- "How do you think using AI affected your understanding of the material?"
- "Do you feel more or less confident in your own abilities after using AI in this way?"

If you frame AI use as a learning decision rather than just a rule-breaking one, students can start to see how shortcuts can compromise their education.

Reinforce Institutional Values

While these conversations help you enforce institutional policies, they also give you an opportunity to shape an academic culture where learning and integrity matter.

- Explore how AI use relates not only to academic honesty but also to the kind of professional integrity students may encounter in their careers.
- Discuss how various fields connected to students' majors are approaching ethical AI use.
- Highlight that responsible engagement with AI is becoming an increasingly valued skill in the workplace.

Promote Accountability and Growth

If a student misused AI, the conversation shouldn't end with punishment. It should end with a plan for improvement. Think about these constructive next steps:

- Revising the assignment transparently, with clear documentation of their process
- Creating a personal action plan for future assignments

These approaches can make sure that conversations about misuse foster academic growth, responsibility, and ethical decision-making. The goal is to prepare students for a world where they must navigate AI thoughtfully and professionally.

DISCUSSION AND ACTIVITY

In this chapter, we've wrestled with the anxiety surrounding AI misuse and the possibility that we're sliding into a mindset of constant surveillance. We've also taken a closer look at the underlying ethical and practical challenges that surface when AI becomes more difficult to detect. The examples of John, Emma, and Alex spotlight how discipline-specific contexts influence the kind of advice educators should offer. What's clear is that assessing students' use of AI goes hand in hand with rethinking how we evaluate their work and whether we're cultivating a genuine culture of integrity.

Discussion

From Policing to Integrity

We spend a lot of time looking for "red flags" that suggest AI misuse and that can unintentionally encourage a gotcha mentality. Rather than relying on external tools or heightened surveillance measures, how might we foster an environment that values honesty from the outset? Could conversations about academic ethics, modeling best practices, and guiding students to reflect on their learning processes prove more effective?

Advising John, Emma, and Alex

Each student's context is unique. Consider the examples of John, Emma, and Alex in the chapter. How would you advise each of these students regarding their AI use? When it comes to this issue, the same approach won't necessarily work for all three. How do varying academic disciplines or student needs shape the advice we give?

Balancing Workplace Skills With Fundamental Knowledge

Whether they're future engineers, teachers, or health care workers, our students will enter job markets saturated with AI tools. They need to know how to use AI responsibly and still master the core skills of their field. How do we make AI a thoughtful supplement to, rather than a substitute for, these core competencies?

Activity

Purpose

While AI detection is still up for debate, we do know that instructors will, at times, have to talk to students about potential AI misuse. This activity gives you a space to practice those conversations in a safe, low-pressure environment, allowing you to refine your communication style.

Task

You'll adopt the role of an instructor and utilize ChatGPT Advanced Voice to simulate a conversation with a student suspected of using AI improperly. If you don't have access to Advanced Voice, you can still use traditional ChatGPT and type your replies. This role-playing activity nudges you to think carefully about tone, clarity, and the kind of questions that lead to productive dialogue.

Start a new chat with ChatGPT and input the starter prompt below verbatim. After it replies, tap on the headphone icon to continue your conversation using Advanced Voice.

Starter Prompt: Hello, I'd like you to take on a persona so that I can practice a tough conversation. I need you to be a 3rd-year computer science student named Jeff. I'll be a faculty member, and you're enrolled in my English composition course. You have a part-time job and are caring for a sick parent at home. I'm questioning you about an assignment that you submitted that I think might be AI-generated. I need you to be slightly aloof and then push back on me when possible.

1. Set the Scenario
   » Outline the student's assignment, the nature of the suspected AI misuse, and your goals for the meeting.
   » Maybe you noticed unusual shifts in writing style or a level of technical detail that doesn't match the student's past work.
2. Experiment with Tones
   » Practice different approaches like empathetic, firm, or inquisitive to see how "Jeff" responds.
   » Consider your nonverbal cues in a real-life classroom or office setting. How might your approach change if you're meeting face-to-face versus online?
3. Document and Reflect
   » Capture ChatGPT's answers so you can review them.
   » How did the conversation shift when you changed tones or asked more open-ended questions?
   » Did the student's "responses" reveal a more honest perspective on AI use, or did they become defensive?
4. Refine Your Communication Style
   » Reflect on which tone or questioning strategy best conveyed your expectations while still exhibiting trust.
   » Consider how you would adapt these conversational strategies with your real students, especially those who feel anxious or misunderstood.

Criteria for Success

You'll know the role-playing activity was successful if:

- You feel prepared and confident when handling sensitive conversations about AI misuse.
- You can articulate AI policies clearly and calmly so that students fully grasp the expectations.
- Your tone and approach lead to open productive dialogue rather than defensiveness or confusion.
- You identify communication strategies that work well and can be applied in real classroom conversations.

Conclusion

Key Takeaways

INTRODUCTION

Thank you for joining me on our walk through the modernized classroom. My hope is that each chapter offered a fresh perspective, inspired a new teaching strategy, or simply reminded you why you first dedicated yourself to helping students learn. By embracing these ideas, you're shaping the future of education.

Below, you'll find a quick-reference guide to the core concepts we've explored. These chapter takeaways provide actionable insights designed to help you make immediate improvements to your teaching practice. Revisit them whenever you need a refresh on effective prompt design, assessment strategies, or integrity frameworks that work in today's classrooms.

FOUNDATIONS OF GENERATIVE AI

Generative AI has fundamentally transformed how we create and process information. Once viewed as science fiction, these technologies now permeate our daily lives, from smartphone assistants to content creation tools. For educators, understanding the building blocks of this technology moves beyond just academic curiosity. It's become essential knowledge that shapes how we teach, assess, and prepare students for a rapidly evolving world. It also marks a fundamental shift from systems that merely classify to ones that create. This power spans text, images, audio, video, and code, revolutionizing education alongside countless other fields.

Essential Concepts

- Machine learning allows AI to improve without explicit programming learning from patterns in data.
- Natural language processing enables AI to understand and generate human language.
- Large language models contain billions of parameters trained on vast text repositories.

- Prompt engineering is the art of crafting effective instructions that guide the output from AI systems.

Understanding how these systems work reveals both their capabilities and limitations. Large language models (LLMs) don't "think" in human terms; they predict word sequences based on statistical patterns learned during training. They excel at tasks involving pattern recognition and text generation but struggle with factual accuracy, mathematical reasoning, and ethical judgment. These limitations become critical considerations when integrating AI into educational settings. Keep in mind these are the limitations of today. Advanced reasoning models will quickly make them a thing of the past.

Success in this environment doesn't come from banning these tools or pretending they don't exist. Instead, it emerges from understanding their fundamental nature and leveraging their strengths thoughtfully to design learning experiences that acknowledge both what AI can do and what remains human about education: connection, mentorship, and the guidance that helps students discover wisdom.

MASTERING PROMPT DESIGN

The prompt is everything. Your ability to craft precise instructions for AI tools will determine whether you get mediocre outputs or high-quality results. What once required technical expertise now demands something different: the skill to communicate clearly with these systems. For you, mastering prompt design is the gateway to harnessing the full potential of AI.

Effective prompt design combines clarity, precision, and context. Vague instructions produce vague results. The more specific and thoughtful your prompts, the more tailored and useful the responses become. Think of it as directing a highly knowledgeable but literal assistant who needs explicit guidance to deliver exactly what you need.

Essential Principles

- Focus on author, audience, and purpose in every prompt.
- Eliminate ambiguity through precise language and clear expectations.
- Provide relevant context that frames its understanding.
- Structure prompts with consistent details and illustrative examples.
- Scale your prompt's complexity to match your task's complexity.

When you tell a student "write better," they rightfully ask "how?" Similarly, telling AI to "make something about cars" yields generic unfocused content. But when you are more specific, it gives the AI the direction it needs to generate valuable, targeted material. When you provide contextual understanding and properly structured prompts, it yields dramatically better results.

As you integrate AI into your practice, it's worth noting that your expertise in communication may now extend to machine interaction as well. The truly valuable skill isn't just knowing what you want but also knowing how to ask for it effectively. Mastering prompt design allows you to transform these tools from a novelty to a powerful ally.

IMPLEMENTING AI IN THE CLASSROOM

When you're integrating AI into your classroom, don't worry so much about having cutting-edge technology. Instead, be more thoughtful about whether it will enhance learning. The Technological Pedagogical Content Knowledge (TPACK) framework provides a clear lens to help AI support your teaching goals rather than dictate them.

Essential Considerations

- Prioritize flexibility; tools should adapt to your teaching style, not force conformity.
- Evaluate total costs including hidden fees that might create access barriers.
- Investigate vendor reputation, reliability, and support systems.
- Review privacy policies thoroughly to understand what student data is collected and how it's used.

Classroom integration should be purposeful. These tools can streamline administrative tasks, generate discussion prompts, provide feedback, and create accessible study materials. They should still align with your pedagogy to be effective.

Implementation challenges are inevitable. You may face limitations like unreliable internet and faculty resistance that often stems from legitimate concerns about academic integrity and classroom dynamics. Address these through structured professional development, stakeholder discussions, and clear institutional policies that balance innovation with academic standards. Maintain a "human in the loop" approach where educators retain oversight and judgment. Create feedback loops incorporating student input and faculty reflection to continuously refine how AI tools are used.

ETHICS, FAIRNESS, AND PERSONALIZED LEARNING WITH AI

The internet contains everything—the good, the bad, and the ugly aspects of human thought and behavior. AI models trained on this ocean of data have learned from both their brilliance and biases that are inherent in how these systems are built. Training data frequently overrepresents certain demographics while underrepresenting others; algorithms learn problematic patterns; and feedback loops amplify existing disparities over time. These biases manifest in real-world consequences: Facial recognition systems misidentify people, predictive models disproportionately target marginalized communities, and language models reinforce gender stereotypes.

Our prompts either reinforce or mitigate these biases. Even neutral-seeming questions about "influential articles" or "key studies" can produce outputs that favor Western perspectives or high-resource institutions. Counteracting these tendencies requires intentional prompt design.

Essential Strategies

- Craft prompts that explicitly request diversity of perspectives and examples.
- Use gender-neutral language and avoid stereotypes in your instructions.
- Include context to discourage oversimplification in AI responses.
- Regularly test and refine prompts to identify and address patterns of bias.
- Apply manual review from diverse perspectives to detect subtle biases.

While addressing bias is essential, AI also creates unprecedented opportunities for personalized learning. LLMs understand context, generate tailored responses, facilitate feedback, and engage in conversational learning. You can leverage these tools to create custom study guides, develop practice questions, offer personalized feedback, provide language support, and facilitate collaborative activities. The most effective approach balances automation with human oversight. While AI excels at generating these materials, you need to review, refine, and align this content with your learning objectives. This "human in the loop" approach helps the technology enhance your presence in the course rather than replace it.

As AI continues to transform education, how we approach it matters. Embedding ethical considerations into every aspect of how we use this technology creates a future where it enhances the human elements of teaching. Our goal is to empower students and build knowledge.

CRAFTING AI-DRIVEN ASSESSMENTS

Traditional assessment models fail in an AI world. We have to shift from measuring final products to evaluating the learning process itself. Forget "AI-proofing" assessments; it creates an untenable situation. Instead, build "AI-informed" evaluations that integrate this technology purposefully into your assessment strategy.

Essential Strategies

- Design multistage assessments with visible thinking checkpoints
- Require students to justify decisions and document their reasoning.

- Create real-world scenarios requiring contextual understanding.
- Include personalized reflection components that resist AI automation.
- Develop collaborative projects that demand adaptive thinking.

The Transparency in Learning and Teaching (TILT) framework transforms vague directives into structured learning opportunities through three key elements. *Purpose*: why students complete the assignment; *Task*: exactly what to do; and *Criteria for Success*: how they'll be evaluated. This clarity becomes vital when explaining how AI may or may not support student work.

Connect assessments to authentic, real-world applications through case studies, scenario-based assignments, and cross-disciplinary projects. When evaluations mirror genuine professional challenges, they demand contextual awareness, ethical judgment, and creative problem solving that is not easy for AI to replicate.

UPHOLDING ACADEMIC INTEGRITY IN THE AGE OF AI

The traditional safeguards of academic integrity such as timed, in-person exams, plagiarism checks, and honor codes weren't designed for a world where students can generate polished essays or solve complex equations in minutes. Rather than fight a battle you have no chance to win with blanket bans or unreliable detection tools, think about how you can establish new frameworks that acknowledge the presence of AI in the educational process and preserve genuine opportunities to learn.

The detection dilemma presents significant challenges. These tools produce false positives that unfairly flag students' original work, creating a particular disadvantage for non-native English speakers. At the same time, they can also generate false negatives that let AI-generated content slip through undetected, which undermines the system's credibility. This technological arms race is one that detection tools consistently lose as AI evolves with more advanced reasoning models. All this highlights the need for a more balanced approach.

Clear, discipline-specific AI policies provide necessary guidance as this landscape evolves. One-size-fits-all approaches fail to address the needs of different fields and courses, which creates confusion among students navigating inconsistent expectations. Effective policies explicitly outline permitted and restricted uses while they provide focus on guidance rather than simply police violations.

Essential Strategies

- Establishing boundaries regarding AI in your syllabus and reinforcing these expectations throughout the semester, especially before major assignments, can help create clarity for students.
- Designing assessments that emphasize process over product can help students document their thinking.

- Considering the incorporation of personal experiences and case-based problems may present research challenges that go beyond AI's capabilities.
- AI-use statements, where students document how they utilized AI tools in their work, might provide valuable transparency.
- Focusing on conversations rather than accusations when addressing potential misuse tends to create more productive outcomes.
- Suspected violations can serve as teachable moments about authentic learning.
- AI policies might be more effective when tailored to specific disciplines, with consideration for different learning objectives within those subjects.

The way forward isn't about creating perfect detection systems or AI-proof assignments. Instead, it focuses on creating a culture of integrity where students understand the value of learning and see AI as a tool to enhance their work rather than replace their thinking. When you approach potential misuse with curiosity instead of accusations, you create opportunities for honest dialogue about responsible AI integration. These are the skills students will need throughout their academic and professional lives.

Remember: "The days of the five-paragraph essay are over." Maintaining academic integrity now depends on our ability to design meaningful assessments that AI can augment but not replace, and to have frank conversations with students about its role in their journey.

FINAL THOUGHTS

Generative AI is here to stay, and it represents a fundamental shift in how knowledge is accessed, created, and shared.

Perhaps the most profound opportunity presented by AI is to consider not what AI can do but how it compels us to reconsider what education should be. For centuries, our educational systems have prioritized information retention and standardized assessment, born in an era when access to knowledge was limited and specialized expertise was scarce. Now, with easy access to AI systems, it forces us to face a pivotal question: What uniquely human capacities should we nurture in our students?

The teacher's job shifts from being the source of knowledge to guiding curiosity, from giving answers to helping students ask better questions. This change takes courage. It means letting go of some control, rethinking how we grade work, and creating classrooms where uncertainty and mistakes are seen as part of the learning process. The best teachers won't just add AI to their toolkit; they'll use this moment to reimagine learning itself and ask not just "How can AI help us teach what we've always taught?" but "What should we teach in a world with access to advanced artificial intelligence?"

Ironically, as machines get smarter, education may become more human in a way that celebrates the messy nature of authentic learning. While AI handles information tasks, we can focus on higher-order thinking while building empathy, creativity, and ethical judgment in our students—all skills needed to use these powerful tools more wisely.

Technology may change how we access knowledge, but our human ability to question, connect, and create meaning will remain at the heart of education. Our job isn't to compete with machines. That's impossible. It's to use them to become more curious, creative, and connected to the questions that make learning worthwhile.

References

Ajjawi, R., Tai, J., Dollinger, M., Dawson, P., Boud, D., & Bearman, M. (2023). From authentic assessment to authenticity in assessment: broadening perspectives. *Assessment & Evaluation in Higher Education*, *49*(4), 499–510. https://doi.org/10.1080/02602938.2023.2271193

Alexander, B. (2020). *Academia next: The futures of higher education*. Johns Hopkins University Press. https://dx.doi.org/10.1353/book.72236

Alexander, B. (2023, June 20). *Launching AI, academia, and the future*. Substack. https://aiandacademia.substack.com/p/launching-ai-academia-and-the-future

Anderson, L. W., Krathwohl, D. R., & Bloom, B. S. (2001). *A taxonomy for learning, teaching, and assessing: A revision of Bloom's Taxonomy of educational objectives*. Longman.

Angwin, J., Larson, J., Mattu, S., & Kirchner, L. (2016, May 23). *Machine bias*. ProPublica. https://www.propublica.org/article/machine-bias-risk-assessments-in-criminal-sentencing

Gordon, R. (2023, March 3). Large language models are biased: Can logic help save them? *MIT News*. https://news.mit.edu/2023/large-language-models-are-biased-can-logic-help-save-them-0303

Hardesty, L. (2018, February 12). Study finds gender, skin-type bias in commercial artificial-intelligence systems. *MIT News*. https://news.mit.edu/2018/study-finds-gender-skin-type-bias-artificial-intelligence-systems-0212

Mishra, P., & Koehler, M. J. (2006). Technological pedagogical content knowledge: A framework for teacher knowledge. *Teachers College Record*, *108*(6), 1017–1054.

Myers, A. (2023, May 15). *AI-detectors biased against non-native English writers*. Stanford University, Human-Centered AI Institute. https://hai.stanford.edu/news/ai-detectors-biased-against-non-native-english-writers

OpenAI. (n.d.). *How can educators respond to students presenting AI-generated content as their own*? OpenAI Help Center. Retrieved February 22, 2025, from https://help.openai.com/en/articles/8313351-how-can-educators-respond-to-students-presenting-ai-generated-content-as-their-own

TILT Higher Ed. (n.d.). *Transparency in Learning and Teaching project*. TILT Higher Ed. Retrieved February 20, 2025, from https://www.tilthighered.com

Winkelmes, M. A. (2013). Transparency in teaching: Faculty share data and improve students' learning. *Liberal Education*, *99*(2), 48–55.

Index

The letter *t* following a page number denotes a table.

About the Author

Nick Gaspar serves as director of online and digital education at the University of Michigan-Flint. Since 2006, he has dedicated his career to advancing educational technology through innovation, thoughtful change management, and accessible digital practices.

As an advocate for generative AI in education, Nick developed the Generative AI Prompt Literacy professional development course. He also codeveloped Teaching with GenAI, an asynchronous course that empowers educators to integrate AI responsibly and effectively. His leadership extends to serving on the University of Michigan's Generative Artificial Intelligence Advisory (GAIA) Committee, shaping university-wide strategies on the ethical use of AI.

The thoughtful integration of technology drives Nick's work. He believes in its power to enhance teaching effectiveness and accelerate student learning. This conviction that educational innovation can expand access and opportunities throughout society led him to cocreate and colead the Teaching with GenAI Learning Communities at both the Flint and Ann Arbor campuses. Faculty and instructional staff gather in these interdisciplinary spaces to explore AI integration collaboratively. They share best practices and develop practical resources with meaningful educational impact. Through these initiatives and beyond, Nick champions technology's potential to broaden higher education's reach and impact for the communities these institutions serve.